Childhood Snippets

Growing Up In Post War Philadelphia

Stephen Robert Goldman

iUniverse books may be ordered through booksellers or by contacting:

iUniverse
1663 Liberty Drive
Bloomington, IN 47403
www.iuniverse.com
1-800-Authors (1-800-288-4677)

ISBN: 978-1-4502-9014-2 (sc)
ISBN: 978-1-4502-9015-9 (ebook)

Printed in the United States of America

iUniverse rev. date: 02/15/2011

*To all who kindly helped or patiently listened – especially
my wife, Terry; sister, Jan; friend, Sam Yosen;
and son, Tim, for the cover artwork*

Contents

Introduction

My growing up years from my birth in 1945 in my homes in Strawberry Mansion and Southwest Philadelphia during and after the Second World War into the 1950's in the West Oak Lane section in Philadelphia were full of fun, excitement and wonderment. These are a few snippets that show some of my experiences during that post-war era of prosperity in the megalopolis in Southeastern Pennsylvania. All of the experiences are true and actually happened. I was directly involved in some, others just happened when I was there to observe them. All in all, they were fun times.

Hopefully, you, the reader, will be reminded of your growing up years and enjoy tripping down memory lane as I often do. I have had the pleasure of reminiscing through the telling of these tales over and over again. Many people have enjoyed listening to my escapades and encounters during my childhood years. Now I have set keyboard to computer and reduced these fond memories to writing for all to enjoy.

Birth, Taxes & Ration Stamps

My mother, Sylvia, told me of when she worked for a candy company wrapping candies to earn a living. She said she was not well liked because she was known at a "rate buster." A person who exceeded the standard number of wraps of candy per hour causing the rate per wrapped candy to lower. Therefore, everyone made less money and had to wrap more candy.

My father, Irving, who hated that he did not have a middle name or initial, mustered out of the army during WWII with a medical discharge having contracted Buerger's Disease by smoking a pipe. He settled in Philadelphia and took a job at Sun Ship Yard in Southeastern Pennsylvania building ships for the war effort.

They met while my father was still in the service through the auspices of my father's sister Rose in Philadelphia. My mother and Rose were close friends. My parents corresponded while my father was still serving his country and was at Camp Shelby, Mississippi in boot camp. After he was a civilian again, they soon married and along I came!

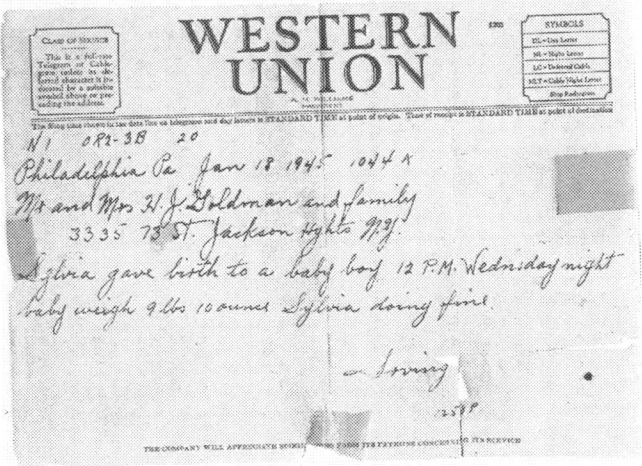

My father sent his folks a telegram about my arrival. Although the telegram he sent his family in Jackson Heights, New York was incorrect as to the time of my birth; it nonetheless announced my birth into the world. According to my mother, I was born at 12:15 a.m. on January 17th, 1945. The telegram mixed PM and night. 12 p.m. being noon and 12 a.m. being midnight. Hoping for a December child and just missing the tax deduction, I was here! They had been hoping for a December child so they would get an extra tax deduction for 1944, but here I was two weeks later and missed the end of year cut off.

They immediately applied for ration stamps in my name. The war still raged on and having an additional ration stamp book meant more of everything that was rationed. I was told a lot of trading of stamps went on. My parents, like most people, didn't own a car, so stamps for gasoline and such were traded for things needed in the household. Even after the war ended, the stamp books were kept "just in case" anything happened.

33rd & Diamond

My earliest childhood memories are of our apartment at 33rd and Diamond Streets in the Strawberry Mansion section of Philadelphia. We lived on the second floor of a walk-up apartment. I have no idea about the occupants of the first and third floors. When I was around the age of two, I fell down one of the two flights of steps. My mother had left the door open from the apartment to the stairway and I, not being familiar with the concept of steps, walked out of the apartment onto the landing. Without knowing or understanding, I walked off the landing and rolled down the stairs. My mother was quite upset. She ran down to get me and found me lying at the bottom of the stairs quite shaken up. I was not hurt nor was I in pain. I just treated it as an interesting experience that I did not wish to repeat.

In the mornings and evenings while I was in the rather small bathroom washing and brushing my teeth, my mother sang to me while she sat on the lid of the toilet watching and encouraging me. She always sang my favorite song - Alice Blue Gown. It must have been a hit around that time. I just loved to listen to her sing and she loved singing it for me.

One evening while I was in the bathroom brushing my teeth, there was knocking at the apartment door. No one had ever knocked on the door before. I went to the door with my mother, who opened it. To my astonishment there were several people in costumes making a lot of noise. My mother explained that it was Halloween and that I was too young to participate. Next year I would be able to go out in a costume like the "older" children and go Trick or Treating. I had no idea what that meant.

On a nearby street there was a very large building with tall white pillars in the front. The pillars or columns were so big around that they could hide me. I played there on occasion while my mother went inside.

In my adulthood, many people questioned my memories of these times. Then, many years later, while visiting my Aunt Rose who now lived in New Haven, Connecticut, I was relating these memories. My first wife and three children were once again making noises about these memories I had. My aunt suddenly got up and left the room. She appeared as abruptly as she had disappeared. In her hand was a photograph of the building with the tall pillars. It was the synagogue across the street from our apartment at 33rd and Diamond in Strawberry Mansion! My early childhood memories are seldom questioned any more.

Ruby Street

One day I woke up and we were all moved in to a new home on Ruby Street in Southwest Philadelphia. I slept through it all or just plain don't remember. Either way, we were there! The house was, if my memory serves me correctly, a 14-foot wide row home. It had 3 bedrooms and a bath upstairs, a living room, dining room and kitchen downstairs. The basement was unfinished including no steps up and out to the backyard. There was just a really steep slab of concrete up to the double doors on the outside. The doors were like those found on old tornado shelters. Behind the house was an alley. Our backyard was fenced in with an iron railing that had curved semicircular loops at the top. The yard was covered with grass. The front of the house had an open porch with a wooden railing across the front, in between our adjacent neighbor's house and ours, and a half railing on the side with the steps to a common stair to the sidewalk. The street was narrow by today's standards. The entire neighborhood was built for horse and buggy days.

No one had a garage. Only one black car was parked on the street and it only moved on Sundays. Of course, being the only car on the street, my ball always got stuck under it between the asphalt paving and the rear differential. You would think, with no cars on the street, I would have plenty of room to play without encountering the only car on the street!

Milk and bread were delivered to your door. The milk wagon was literally a milk wagon drawn by a horse that followed the milkman and knew his route as well as he did. It was a treat when the horse came down the street following the milkman. Starting and stopping at each house while the milk was placed on the doorsteps of the houses. Once in a while I got to feed the horse. Usually it was an apple. The milkman would always tell me to keep my hand open wide so the horse wouldn't accidentally bite my hand or fingers. It amazed me that the horse ate the apple, seeds and all!

The mailman came every day with the mail for the street. He would come around lunchtime and would open the olive drab relay box, sit down on the inside bottom and proceed to eat his lunch.

...an iron railing that had curved semicircular loops at the top.

Grandma Gussie and me

My father's mother, Gussie, came to visit on occasion. Grandma always had her black Brownie camera with her. It took 620 black & white film. She never missed an opportunity to take pictures of the family. Never scenery; always the family!

Climbing Out of the Crib

My mother didn't work and liked to sleep later than the working folks. She kept me in my crib as a means of control and out of trouble. Like most people, I didn't like being confined or restricted. But I outsmarted her. Sometime after the age of two I decided I didn't like being cooped up in the crib any more. So I just climbed over the railing and down onto the floor. I was free!

This made my parents realize that I needed a real bed and that the days of keeping me restricted were over. I was allowed to sleep on the studio couch in the third bedroom. I had to put the cushions from the back of the couch on the floor in case I fell out. I wasn't used to sleeping in a bed without a side guard to keep me in.

Once I actually fell off the studio couch onto the cushions. It scared me and I cried for some time. My parents just ignored me. I suppose they had learned to tell the difference between my crying for attention and a cry that I was serious. I wasn't happy about not getting any attention and quickly got over it. I climbed back into be and went to sleep once more.

I was free to roam the house at will. I must have been a good child because I didn't get into things nor was I destructive. The thought of going out of the house never entered my mind. I just went downstairs and played. From then on the playpen I was usually kept in went unused until the arrival of my brother sometime later.

Hobbyhorse

Around the time of my transitioning from a crib to a bed I had a fantastic hobbyhorse. It was made of a leaf of spring steel several inches wide and had a 45-degree angle bend at the midpoint. This spring steel leaf was painted bright green and was attached to a colorfully painted wooden base for stability. On the top part of the spring was a wooden seat that had a stylized horse head attached to the front of it. The seat and horse head were painted in wonderful bright colors. I have never seen one like it since.

I would climb upon the seat and bounce up and down for long periods of time. My imagination ran wild. I thought about riding like a cowboy through herds of cattle. I imagined going through wooded areas and onto large plains. It was a wonderful and adventurous time.

The hobbyhorse was kept in the basement under the front windows. It was a convenient place to play with and store the toy. In the warm weather the basement was cool and comfortable. In the colder weather, being near the coal furnace, it was warm.

One day, while I was playing and bouncing up and down, there was a very loud snap followed by my falling with a bang to the base of the toy. This was followed by great pain in my bottom. The steel spring had snapped in two at the bend and I was no longer in possession of a fantastic hobbyhorse. No more adventures while riding and bouncing up and down. I was sad for a while, but soon got over it. After all, I had many other toys with which to play.

Along Came Ed

During the time of our living at 33rd and Diamond and now on Ruby Street, my mother would sit on the floor and play games with me. We played with Tinkertoy, Lincoln Logs, building blocks, Pick Up Stix and the like. She told me stories about her and her family. She explained that I was named after her mother, my grandmother Sarah, who was no longer alive. It was ingrained in me that we were Bristol heirs. Something I didn't understand at the time partly because I thought the word was air and not heir. I later learned that the family name on one side was Bristol and we were suppose to inherit something, but never actually did. It was a fun time when she played with me while sitting on the floor, but then the time came when she couldn't sit on the floor with me.

My mother, a heavyset woman, began to prepare me for the arrival of the new baby. She didn't know the sex of the baby before hand. Those things weren't possible then. So she just explained in a somewhat excited manner that I was going to have a brother or sister. She said that she was going to go away for a while and that my Grandmother (Gussie) would be there to take care of me.

She must have done a good job because I was so excited about the new arrival and just couldn't wait. I kept asking if it was time for the baby to come. What did I know about pregnancy and birth at the age of three!

Time passed and Grandma came. My mother disappeared. Then one afternoon, my father took me to pick up my mother and Ed in the hospital. It was an interesting time in the lobby of the hospital. My new baby brother was brought out in a covered wheeled cloth hamper-like cart. They lifted the top and swung it back and down on its hinges to reveal my brother Ed. They called him "Whitey" because of his thin white hair.

I was so impressed. I had a new baby brother!

Once we were home, everyone's attention was focused on Ed. I learned about diapers, bathing, feeding and the general care of babies. Lots of people came to visit and brought presents for the baby. They liked to stare at the baby in the crib that was decorated with decalcomanias.

I remember watching my father and learning about decalcomanias and how they slid easily onto the side of the crib after being soaked in warm water. It was simply amazing.

Never again would my mother sit on the floor with me and play. She only ever sat on a chair and talked with me. I was so disappointed, but never complained or said a word. Life was good.

Jars of Sand

My best friend, Ira, lived up the street from me on the same side. We were very close. As close as 4-year olds can get. We played together and went places together.

One day Ira and I decided to collect sand in glass jars. I don't know why we collected the sand. But, we did. Sand was not very prevalent for some reason. Dirt was. So we decided to collect sand. I collected more sand than Ira. Ira kept stealing my sand and putting it in his jar. I collected more and he kept taking it. I was unhappy about this and told Ira that if he took sand from my jar one more time that I would break the jar over his head. I don't know what possessed me to say such a thing. After all, he was my best friend. We spent hours that day collecting sand. It amounted to about a pint all together. He had gathered less than half of what I did. Then, suddenly, he once again had way more sand in his jar than I had in mine. I took my glass jar and raised it over his head. Then I smashed it as hard as I could onto his head. He screamed and cried. The blood ran all down his face. It was horrible. He ran home. I walked home.

I told my mother what I had done. She called his mother and they talked for a bit. I was punished. Ira and I were no longer best friends. Just friends.

Buerger's Disease

My father worked for a sheet metal fabrication company. He was a shear operator. A shear is, effectively, a very large and strong scissor that cuts sheet metal into sizes needed to fabricate parts. He had wooden machinist's tool chest handcrafted of wood and lined with green felt and full of machinist's tools that he periodically brought home.

A couple of evenings a week he went to night school to further his education. He was studying engineering to improve his knowledge of mechanics. He used a slide rule to do his mathematics work along with the books for the classes.

My father suffered terribly from Buerger's Disease due to his former pipe smoking days. Because of the disease, my father was not allowed to smoke; had to wear only white sox as the dyes used then could go into his body through his skin; and was not allowed to be exposed to the sun on the beach. When we later went down the shore, he only wore street clothes on the beach and never went in the water.

I remember several weekday afternoons when he stayed home from work because of the pain caused by poor flow in the peripheral arteries and veins in his legs and feet. The doctor would come to treat his condition. My mother made me sit outside on the open porch and wait until he was done with his visit with my father. During these times, my father would scream so loud that you would think he was being killed. My mother explained that the doctor was giving him injections in his feet and they were very painful.

When it was all over, I was allowed back in the house but had to stay away from father who was now sleeping. I generally stayed downstairs and played.

Clock Wires and Dead Outlet

From about the age of four years old, wires and electricity fascinated me. My mother gave me a small old wooden cased mantle clock to play with. I had two long wires and plug. I would connect the wires to the plug from the clock by wrapping the bare copper conductors around the prongs of the plug. I ran the wires in a long string across the living room floor into the dining room and had the second plug connected at the end. I was allowed to plug the assemblage into an outlet in the dining room floor and pretend the thing worked and did all sorts of things. Imagination was an important part of my life during this playtime. The outlet in the floor of the dining room was close to the party wall and was "dead." Therefore, according to my mother, I wouldn't get hurt and could not do any damage.

Knowing what I know now about electricity, it frightens me to think about what I was doing in my childhood days with this wiring. Today I know that a non-operating outlet results from more than just not being connected to the power main. This was the age before three-prong grounded outlets. There were only two slots in the round single outlet in the floor. It is possible that the narrow slot or hot side of the outlet was still connected to the main and was hot or live with the wide neutral slot not being connected. This would render the outlet still inoperable – appearing to be a dead outlet. However, it would be very dangerous and enable the possibility of electric shock or worse, electrocution! My parents had no clue.

The Telephone Repairman

Like most Jewish women of the time, my mother was a Yenta – an old Jewish gossip. Though not old, definitely a gossip. She could talk for hours with her sister, cousins, friends or anyone. I have no idea what she talked about, but she could talk. She told stories. Complained. Explained, and, just went on and on.

Most of this time was spent on the telephone. Then, one day the phone stopped working! It was a disaster. Being the only telephone in the house meant that she had to go to a neighbor's house, get permission to use the phone to call the phone company and report the trouble. This was a major undertaking.

Waiting for the repairman was another unwanted task. Then, like now, they couldn't tell you when the person would come. You had to wait and wait and wait. Finally, the repairman came. He was wearing work clothes that were indicative of a telephone repairman of the era - grey work pants and a flannel Carhartt style work shirt. He arrived in a panel truck that had Bell System printed on the side with a stylized telephone for the logo. It was a cool thing to see, as trucks never came down our street.

The repairman was equipped with a leather tool belt and all kinds of wonderful tools and gadgets. Best of all, he had a portable handset clipped to the bottom of the holster, which had a dial and wires with clips that could connect directly to the telephone line at any junction box. He could call from anywhere to anywhere. He used it to test the line for a dial tone. Once he decided the circuit was in working order, he proceeded to take out a long, straight blade screwdriver and take the telephone apart. This was just wonderful. I got to see the insides of the telephone!

It was amazing when he took off the cover. The screws that held the telephone together didn't fall out of the cover. They were somehow made to stay with the cover and not get lost. After the cover was off, he proceeded to take a part out of the phone. Then he went out to his truck to get a new part. He installed the new part in the telephone and put the cover back on. I don't know how he knew what to change. But he knew, nevertheless. He called a number that produced a loud tone to test the phone. Then he did the most amazing thing. He dialed another set of only four numbers, normally there were seven, and hung up. The telephone rang. He made it ring and no one had called. This was about the most terrific thing I had ever seen. I asked him what he did, but he wouldn't tell me. He said he wasn't allowed to tell anyone the secret numbers.

Many years later I learned the code by watching a repairman carefully as he dialed the numbers. Rotary phones were easy because they were slow, you could see which hole in the dial the person's finger went into and you could count the clicks the telephone made.

Watching the repairman was probably the best experience I had ever had. It involved electricity. It involved mechanical things. It involved taking things apart to see how they worked, putting them back together again and having them actually function properly. It was just great!

Candlestick Extension Phone

There came a time when my mother was inconvenienced by having to go downstairs from the second floor to answer the telephone. She didn't want to be able to make calls from the upstairs, but just didn't want to have to go downstairs to answer the phone. At some point my parents decided to have an extension telephone installed upstairs. Extension telephones were a big deal, as many people didn't even have a telephone.

Back then the rule was to let the number ring seven times to allow the called party time to answer. Most people let it ring for more. There were no answering machines or Caller ID. So, if no one answered, there were no messages or indication of a call.

In those days, the telephone repairman was also an installer. He came with his tool belt of tools and gadgets and drilled holes in the walls and ran wires from the second floor hallway all the way to the basement. He hooked up the wires to the demarcation block in the basement where the line came in and connected a candlestick telephone to the other end upstairs in the hallway. The candlestick telephone had a place where the dial should be, but it was just a blank circle of black and white.

Now, when the telephone rang, it rang in two places and could be heard upstairs and downstairs at the same time. It was incredible. My mother no longer had to run downstairs to answer the telephone when it rang. Of course, when she was in the basement doing laundry and other things, nothing had changed. She still ran upstairs to answer the phone or just let it ring.

Having an extension gave my mother even more to brag about. She just loved to tell people about her new extension telephone in the upstairs hall. It was just wonderful.

Coal Heat

Our home on South Ruby Street near 54th and Florence in Southwest Philly was heated by a coal furnace. It was cast iron and had the usual doors with vents to adjust the airflow and burn rate of the coal. It had a grate inside that allowed the ashes to fall to the bottom of the furnace and be separated from the burning coal in the upper chamber.

My father shoveled coal from the coal bin on the opposite side of the basement into the furnace and lit it with burning newspaper. He or my mother would periodically stoke the burning coal to allow the ashes to drop through the grate and let more air go through it. Once a day or more frequently on really cold days during the fall and winter, the ashes had to be removed from the bottom of the furnace with a shovel and stored alongside the coal bin in metal buckets or shissels (shissel is a Yiddish word meaning basin or bowl). Coal was added every evening before my parents went to bed to keep the furnace burning overnight. My father complained bitterly about having to get up in the middle of the night to tend to the furnace because it had gone out.

Coal was delivered in large sectioned dump trucks. Each section of the truck represented a full or partial delivery depending on how much coal was ordered. The driver backed the truck up to the front basement window of our house and connected a chute from the truck's rear chute door through the basement window to the coal bin. The chute was in sections and had to be assembled and disassembled on site. This way the coal went directly into the bin in our basement. He then raised the dump bin on the truck, opened the chute door and moved the coal into the chute with a shovel. If more than one section of the dump bin was needed, he removed the wooden separator and pushed the coal with his shovel into the chute. Sometimes the dump bin had to be moved higher at a greater angle to move the coal from the front to the rear of the dump truck bin.

The coal made great whooshing sounds as it moved over the steel truck bin, made its way down the chute and piled up in the basement coal bin. Nothing else made the same sounds. It was like a signature sound for the coal when it was dumped. The smell of the coal was very distinctive, too. It could not be mistaken for anything other than coal.

On Tuesdays the city trucks came to haul the ashes away. My father pushed them up and out the front basement windows. Once all the shissels were put through the windows, he went upstairs and out front to move them toward the curb for collection. The ashes were various shades of dark and light grey with orange colored pieces mixed throughout. Sometimes a clinker was in with them. It was a larger chunk of material that didn't burn and made a clinking sound when it fell through the grate in the furnace.

A salesman came to our house to tell my parents about the modern use of oil heat that was replacing the coal in home heating furnaces. It was a low cost means of doing away with the coal, the ashes and, most important, the need to tend the furnace. Apparently my parents liked the idea and had an oil burner installed.

After the furnace was thoroughly cleaned out, the burner assembly was fitted and cemented to the coal furnace. Electricity was wired to it. No changes were made to the chimney, which allowed the burnt fumes to escape to the outside above the roofline. A 275-gallon oil tank was installed under the window in the front of the basement where the ashes used to be taken out. Pipes were fitted through the front wall of the basement to the outside from the tank. These were used to fill the tank and allow the driver to listen to a whistle sound when the tank was filling. When the whistle made by the exhausting air during tank filling changed pitch or stopped, the driver knew the tank was full. A thermostat was installed in the living room with a wire connecting it to the new oil heater downstairs. It remotely controlled the heater and kept the house at a uniform temperature – 72 degrees! The oil tank was filled. The heater was turned on. Heat went all over the house and no one had to do anything. It was all simply amazing.

Locomotive

In the dining room of our house against the wall was stored a grey steel toy locomotive. It had wheels that were large to support its own weight and that of an occupant. It was rather large as I could get into it and push it and myself around with my feet. I could also sit on the roof of the engine cab, but then my feet didn't reach the floor. I used to ride around the living room and dining room pushing myself forward, backwards and turning the locomotive by moving my weight from one side or the other. I didn't get into it very often, but when I did, I enjoyed being the engineer of an imaginary train. Sometimes it was a passenger train, other times a freight train. Mostly it was just me and the locomotive.

Then, a time came that it no longer interested me and just sat stored against the dining room wall. It blended in to the woodwork, so to speak. I knew it was there, but paid it no mind. So there it sat for months and months.

One day a renewed interest in the locomotive sparked my enthusiasm. Wow, I had almost forgotten about this great toy and the adventures it brought. I began to climb into the cab to sit down. But it had somehow gotten smaller. I pushed and wiggled my way into the cab and finally was able to sit. And, then I realized how tight and uncomfortable I was. I must have grown. I must have grown a lot. The locomotive was now quite small.

I started to get out. I couldn't get out. I was stuck. Being made of heavy gauge steel, there was no flexibility to the toy. Was I to remain here forever? Panic set in. I pushed and squeezed and pulled. Inch by inch my body began to come out.

It hurt as the pressure began to build and my body was scraped through my clothes by the edges of the toy. I was scared. Did I mention that I was scared? Finally, I got out. Shaking and terrified I sat down on the roof of the engine and regained my composure. What an experience. I was growing and didn't realize it. My mother knew I was growing because my clothes and shoes were different. My eating had increased. But, for me, everything seemed the same until I got stuck in the locomotive.

I played with it by sitting on the roof now and pushing it around with my feet. They now reached the floor and I was able to have more adventures being the engineer and driving the trains.

Bed, Doctor and Medicine

After dinner one evening I went to my room and began playing the new phonograph my parents bought for me. It had an electric operated turntable with a mechanical acoustical speaker about an inch and half in diameter. The turntable was just one speed, 78 RPM. The speaker worked by placing a steel phonograph needle in the assembly and fastening it with a thumbscrew. Then you placed a record on the turntable, turned on the motor, put the needle in the outside groove of the record and it began to play. I had only one record and I played each side over and over again.

About this time I began to feel ill. I was having pain in my abdomen and told my mother about it. She promptly telephoned the doctor who came after I had gone to bed. Doctors, pediatricians in particular, still made house calls.

The doctor looked me over and discussed my condition with my parents. My mother was quite worried. He managed to calm her down and allay her fears. I only had a cold and an upset stomach. He suggested a new product he had been using, Coricidin. It was used to treat colds. I was given one tablet with a glass of water and put back to sleep.

The next morning my mother gave me another tablet and went out of the room to get a glass of water so I could easily swallow the tablet. But I fooled her. Because the tablet had a smooth coating, I was able to swallow it without water and did so. When she returned she handed me the water, which I refused. I told her I had swallowed the medicine already and didn't need the water.

She asked how I was feeling. I said I was better and went about the business of once again playing with my new record player.

Sitting in the Dark and Sparks

It was a Saturday morning. My mother scrubbed the laundry on a scrub board in the basement sink and carefully placed it in the shissel. She then went upstairs and out into the back yard. She opened the two doors to the cellar. Then she came back down into the basement, lifted the shissel full of wash onto the floor and proceeded to drag it up the steep slope through the open doors to the back yard. She carefully hung the clothes on the clotheslines to dry. She used wooden poles that had a "V" cut in one end to prop up the sagging clotheslines so the heavy wet clothes didn't touch the ground. She climbed back down the slope to the basement.

Today was different. She left the doors open allowing the sunlight to come into the basement. But, it was still rather dark.

My father was gathering tools and moving things around in the basement. My mother moved a Shaker style bench near the slope to the doors. We sat down on the bench and watched my father work. He was going to do some electrical work in the fuse box. I don't remember what he was doing or why. But the lights went out in the basement when he took out the main fuse. He turned on a flashlight and proceeded to move it around until it was steady on the place he was going to work. This is why the cellar doors remained open letting sunlight in the basement. Otherwise, it would have been pitch black down there.

Still having no idea what was going on with the fuse box, there was suddenly a shower of sparks like fireworks shooting from it. Tiny molten balls of metal showered all over and rolled along the basement floor. When the glow of the sparks stopped, the tiny metal balls seemed to disappear. What a spectacular show!

My mother became upset and was concerned for my father's safety. I had no clue how dangerous the situation was. The possibility of electrocution never entered my mind, as I was unaware of the possibility and its very existence. I had no idea what electricity was or could do. My father was fine. He continued doing whatever it was he was doing. Then, another shower of sparks flew across the room. Wow! We were just far enough away that it didn't reach us. Finally, after about an hour, my father was done his electrical work, put the fuse back in and the basement lights came on. Dad cleaned up his tools and materials. Mom swept the floor. I went upstairs and played in the living room. The fireworks were over. What a show!

Scrub Board and Steps

It wasn't long after the electric sparks incident that my father was down in the basement once more. The doors up to the backyard were wide open and my father was measuring the slope from the basement to the doors along the slope itself. He used a wooden fold-up ruler, which was quite popular then. It was 72 inches long when completely unfolded. Tape measures were very expensive and not in wide spread use.

In the meantime, my mother was doing laundry. Laundry, no matter how young or old you are, never seems to end. There she was washing away at the scrub board in the sink. It was a very hard job, but she did it with unwavering effort.

My father was building steps up the slope to make life easier for my mother. He had purchased lumber and proceeded to cut it up with a hand saw and, using a hammer and nails, assembled the steps that would allow my mother the joy of not having to drag the shissel full of clothes up the steep incline. It took my father several hours to complete the task of making the steps. When they were done, they were a pride and joy to behold. Imagine all the years of dragging and climbing and dragging and climbing that had gone before. Now, you just walked up the steps and out into the yard. My mother was so happy.

Then, another thing happened that changed her life forever. A ringer washing machine was delivered and set up in the basement! No more scrub board. No more hand washing and wringing the laundry. No more hands in the soapy wash water. The wringer was even driven by the motor in the washing machine. No cranking the ringer like other older models required. Just move the lever to make the wringer turn and push the clothes into it and the water was squeezed out. Then the laundry went into the shissel and was carried up the new steps and outside where it was hung on the clotheslines.

Sometime later, while I was watching my mother use her new washing machine, she went to lift up the brown glass bottle of Clorox bleach to put it away on the shelf. It slipped out of her hand and went crashing onto the table and shattered splashing bleach all over my dungarees. She let out a scream and rushed me upstairs to get my clothes off and wash me all over. I was really fine, but I didn't understand what bleach did to your skin. She did.

Later the next day, I looked at my dungarees and saw that the bleach had eaten large moth-like holes all over the upper part. It was really a sight to see. I was amazed and imagined that I might have looked like that had it not been for my mother's quick thinking.

Bathing in a Shissel

Being young and small had many advantages. The most memorable was going swimming in the back yard on hot summer days. My mother brought a shissel and a board into the back yard. She placed the shissel on the grass in the center of the fenced in yard. It was the same one she used for carrying her laundry in and out of the house. She filled it most of the way up with cool water and placed the board across one side. I bathed in this makeshift swimming hole for hours and hours in the heat of the summer day. I used the board as a seat when I wasn't in the water. My mother stayed with me to make sure nothing happened. Nothing ever did.

As I grew older, I grew bigger. There came a time, as with the locomotive, when I was no longer was able to fit in the tub with the board. I was disappointed at not being able to go bathing in the back yard. However, I was pleased that I was growing up – getting bigger, that is.

First Haircut

For the longest time my mother cut my hair. I didn't know any better so that was the way things were. Then, one day I was taken to the barber shop around the corner. It was crowded with grownup men waiting their turn in the barber chair. There were two barbers working there. One barber had his customer almost lying down and was shaving their face. The other was giving someone a haircut.

The barbers were pleased to see my mother and me and greeted us with pleasantries. We sat down in a couple of the chairs that lined the side and front of the barbershop. There were great big windows on the two sides that let in a lot of light. There were magazines and newspapers on all the flat surfaces in front of the windows. Some of the men waiting their turn were reading magazines.

One by one each waiting man was groomed by one of the barbers. They all looked very nice when they were finished. The barber would first cover them over with a large cloth and begin working their magic on their hair. Except for the men who were bald, everyone seemed to get the same haircut. In later years this style would be known as the Kennedy haircut after President John F. Kennedy.

It was my turn, now. The barber put a wooden board with a cushion across the arms of the barber chair. He then motioned for me to come and climb onto the seat. I did. Both the barber and my mother were concerned that I would be scared and cry. I didn't. I was curious about everything and everyone there. It was a new experience – an adventure. The barber helped me up onto the cushion and covered me with a big cloth. He began to cut my hair. The sound of the scissors was interesting. It wasn't what I was used to with a pair of scissors. They went much more rapidly than just cutting paper with one cut at a time.

Soon my hair was all cut and nice. The barber took off the cloth and brushed me all over with a whiskbroom. Another new experience. He made sure all of the cut hairs that were not caught by the cloth were off of me and on the floor. Then he got a big broom and swept all the hair into one place, picked up the pile in a dustpan and placed it all in a trashcan.

My mother paid the barber. We said our goodbyes and went home. From then on I went to the barber for a haircut. Never again would my mother cut my hair. I was a big boy now!

On The Way to Aunt Pearl

One day my mother decided to go visit her sister, my Aunt Pearl. We lived in Southwest Philly and Aunt Pearl lived in West Philly. We had to go on several trolley cars as well as walk quite a bit. We left our house on Ruby Street, walked to the trolley car stop and waited for the first trolley or streetcar to come. It finally arrived and stopped to let us on. My mother paid the operator and we sat down on seats near the center door. After a while, my mother pulled the cord that sounded the buzzer letting the operator know we wanted to get off at the next stop. We got up and stood in front of the center double folding doors and waited. The trolley slowed and came to a stop. My mother and I stepped down. The distance from the bottom step to the street was too high for me so my mother got off, turned around and lifted me off the step onto the street.

We walked to the curb and waited for the next car to come. The trolley came down the street perpendicular to the one we were on and stopped. The operator or motorman, as he was sometimes called, got off the car. He was carrying a large metal rod, which he stuck into the trolley track at a switch and moved the rails to the opposite side of the switch allowing the trolley to make the turn toward us. Once the switch was thrown, the motorman hopped back on the car, closed the doors and moved it to the place where we were waiting. The doors opened, my mother gave the operator some colored paper (transfer) and we moved to the center of the car and sat down.

A short while later, my mother again pulled on the cord to signal the operator of our desire to get off. We again moved in front of the center doors in preparation to exit. The car came to an abrupt stop. We stepped down, my mother stepped off, turned to lift me off and the doors closed. The trolley car jerked forward and began moving down the street. I had no idea what was going on so I just stood there.

Apparently the motorman couldn't see little me in the mirrors and assumed that we had both gotten off. In the meantime, my mother was running after the trolley screaming at the top of her lungs to get anyone's attention she could to make the trolley car stop. Three blocks later the car stopped. In Philadelphia, a block is about one tenth of a mile, so my mother ran almost a third of a mile chasing the streetcar.

My mother had words with the motorman. The center doors once again opened and there was my mother lifting me off as though nothing had happened. We walked a few streets to Aunt Pearl's house for our visit.

I was oblivious to the happenings. For my mother, like any parent, it was a living nightmare.

Fire Engine Ride

On summer afternoons for a dime you could ride one of the many truck-mounted rides that came around. One ride in particular was a real fire engine. It came once a week and stopped at various street locations to load and unload children. It had a red interior and exterior; a ladder hanging on each side; a siren and a bell; and bench seats down the inside center of the length of the engine. The very same seats that real firemen used while on their way to real fires!

My mother would give me a dime to give to the driver or his assistant as payment for the ride. I climbed onto the engine and sat down next to other children who came to ride. Once everyone was sitting down (no seatbelts in those days), we were off for a loud noisy ride around the block. The siren wailed and the bell clanged. It was a wonderful time. Imagine riding in a real fire engine with all that commotion going on.

Once we came back to where we started, those of us children who lived on this part of Ruby Street got off. The ride was over. But, bragging rights went on for a long time. We couldn't wait until next week when it would come once more.

For no known reason, after several weeks of getting to ride on the fire engine, it no longer came. We all waited and waited, but no fire engine. After a few weeks, we gave up on expecting it to show. Life went on. No one seemed to care any more. I missed it.

Many, many years later, in the latter part of the 1980's, when I had my manufacturing business, Wizard 'Lectronics, Inc., in Lansdowne, Pennsylvania, my landlord, who operated a trucking company on the rear part of the property, would come to talk with me. He told me many stories of his time in the Second World War and of his gambling in Atlantic City. One day he started talking about his teenage years. He said that when he was in his late teens he had an avid interest in cars that remained with him to the present time. He used to frequent junkyards and get parts to fix up a car he had. He came across an old fire engine in one junkyard and inquired as to its condition and availability. Lo and behold, it was in running condition. No one wanted it because it was a fire engine and a rather old one at that.

So, he purchased the fire engine, cleaned and fixed it up, and began to go around West Philadelphia giving rides to children for ten cents. He spent many hours one summer making a good living with his fire engine.

I couldn't believe what I was hearing. I told him I used to ride on his fire engine when I was a child. His eyes sparkled with joy! He asked how I liked it and I told him it was just wonderful.

I asked him why he stopped coming as we all missed riding on it, especially me. He said that one day one of the parents asked him if he had insurance. Having no clue what the person was talking about and not really caring as teenagers are wont, he told the truth and said no. After finding out what was involved and realizing he should have insurance, but couldn't afford it, he returned the fire engine to the junkyard. That was the end of the great rides on the fire engine.

It took from the late 1940's until the late 1980's to find out what happened! Some forty years of my life to solve the mystery.

Mirrors in the Truck

At one end of our street was a grocery store in the basement of the corner house. The entrance was on the side of the building facing the street perpendicular to Ruby Street. The people there were nice and treated me with respect. Of course, being between three and four years old, I really didn't know about such a concept. In retrospect, the fact that they even acknowledged my presence was amazing.

On occasion, my mother sent me to the corner grocery store to get one or two items. Being allowed to do things on my own at such an early age was, in and of itself, quite unusual. But, times were different then and being as they were, most children that age were given more latitude than now. I got to know the people at the store and they got to know me. Often I would just go there and look around.

Of the numerous truck-mounted rides that came around my neighborhood was a large enclosed one that had the inside walls all mirrored. There was a ladder to climb up to get into the inside. One day it was parked outside the grocery store and open for business. This "ride" only cost a nickel. Wow! I got to go inside and experience the ride for five cents.

I gave the man my nickel and climbed up the steps into the body of the truck. I was surrounded by mirrors. No matter which way I looked, it looked the same. It was a bright, sunshiny day and no matter which way I looked, it looked like where I came from, which was also the way out. I was allowed to stay for a short time and was told my time was up and I had to get off. I was all turned around and wasn't sure which way was out. The man got me oriented and helped me down to the street.

To this day I am unsure of which way I actually went to get off. As an adult, I understand about the mirrors and the illusion. When I was a child, it was all so real and disconcerting. Did I go into another dimension, or did I really return from whence I came?

More Sparks

My father came home carrying a large box all wrapped up in brown paper and tied up with string. He was excited. My mother apparently already knew what it was. I was taken into the dining room where he unwrapped the box to reveal a set of American Flyer electric trains. Up until now I only had two kinds of trains. One was the kind that had to be pushed around without any track. The other was made in post war Japan of metal and painted by silkscreen with a little mountain. It was a tiny train with a clockwork mechanism that had to be wound up. It would go around an indentation in the metal that had tracks painted on it. When it went into the tunnel in the mountain, it made a lot of whirring sounds, stayed there for a while and then came out.

My father proceeded to set up the circle of track on a round side table in the dining room. It was a bit larger than the train tracks and was suited just fine. He put the track clip on the track, hooked up the wires from the transformer to it and plugged the transformer into the outlet in the wall. He unpacked the locomotive and each car, setting them on the track and coupling them together. On went the power and around and around went the little freight train on the two-rail track. Just like the real thing. It was wonderful!

My mother came in to see the excitement and complained about all of the sparks coming from the wheels of locomotive on the track. These were tiny sparks compared to the ones that came from the electrical box in the basement when my father was working on it. He allayed her fears and explained that it was OK.

I was only allowed to play with the train when one of my parents was there. Otherwise, it had to be unplugged from the wall and not used. I spent many an hour playing with the train. Making it go back and forth, and stop for freight and maintenance. My imagination ran wild.

Television

In the late 1940's television was all the rage. People stood in the windows of television stores and watched what was on the TVs in the window. It was a new and novel medium of communication. No more would you just listen on the radio. You could now see what was happening and watch with delight. The age of electronics was in full swing and everyone wanted to be part of it. Radio had been around for some time now, yet still wasn't mundane. But TV, wow!

In the Winter-Spring time period of 1948 we got a television. We were the second family on our block to have one. It had a 7-inch round picture tube that produced a small rectangular picture on its screen. The television cabinet was made of wood, was very large and heavy. We had an antenna installed on the roof of the house to pick up the signals from the stations. There were only three stations in Philadelphia – WPTZ Channel 3, WFIL Channel 6, and WCAU Channel 10. They only sent signals out in the afternoon and early evening. Programs that I remember watching were Bert Parks and Name That Tune, Milton Berle, Arthur Godfrey, and Howdy Doody.

The TV had to "warm up" when it was turned on. Unlike the solid state "instant on" products of today, these had lots of vacuum tubes that had to heat up before they could work including the picture tube itself. If you wanted to watch a particular program at a particular time, you turned it on a few minutes ahead of time to allow the warm up period to elapse so you could see the show you wanted from the beginning. It took as much as three minutes sometimes for it to warm up.

Some people always had neighbors coming to their home to watch television. We didn't experience that much. Once in a while people came to watch our TV.

Being a youngster, I went to bed early and listened to the shows until I fell asleep. In the morning, there was just an Indian head test pattern on the screen and a steady tone on every channel. There was just snow and static on the channels that didn't have anything.

Television created another market all by itself. There were overlays that had three bands of color to make the picture look like it was in color. I never understood this. It just made each third of the picture from top to bottom a different color. But, people liked it and it sold. Another favorite was putting a magnifying glass in front of the screen. Some fit into the opening and others were the type that were filled with water and mounted on a stand to support the weight. The problem with the magnifying lenses is that you couldn't see the entire picture at most viewing angles. But, they too, sold like hot cakes.

My parents were so proud to own a television in a time when most people couldn't afford one. It cost $400.00 at a time when most people earned $35.00 to $40.00 a week. I never thought of us as rich and apparently we weren't, but we had a TV!

2¢ Broadway Show

Not long after we got our television set, summer came along. Our next-door neighbor's children decided that they would put on a Broadway stage show. Of course it wasn't really Broadway and, except for the songs, many liberties were taken. They cobbled together a stage with props and a makeshift curtain that actually worked. All of the children from the neighborhood were invited along with some of their friends and relatives. Just enough to fill their basement area set aside for an audience. It was complete with chairs set up with an aisle down each side. I knew the set up because I was allowed down their basement that morning with my mother for a sneak preview of how the basement was arranged.

My parents were invited along with some of the other parents. To say the least, there were several adults present. I suppose to both see the show and tend to their children. Little kids can get out of hand, if you didn't know!

We were asked to bring two pennies for each child attending so that their children would feel like it was a real show. We each went into the house next-door, down into the basement after paying our 2¢ and found a seat in the audience.

Some of the basement lights went out and the show began. I have only vague memories of the performance, but I do remember that the sister and brother who were putting on the show performed one of the popular songs of the time. They were "older" children, although still in elementary school. They performed *On the Sunny Side of the Street*, a 1930's song, which was introduced in a Broadway musical many years before.

I imagined a guy and a gal walking around New York City, the place where my father was born and raised, singing along the way on the sunny side of the street. It was a great performance by my neighbors and we all had a wonderful time. When it was over, refreshments were served and we all went home. For me, it was straight off to bed.

Aunt Bess' Lettuce

That summer found me having lunch at my Aunt Bess' house in the next block of Ruby Street. Aunt Bess, who was really my Great Aunt, was the sister of my mother's mother, Sarah, for whom I was named. To get to her house, even though it was the next block, I had to go to the end of my block, go across the cross street, joggle right and then left onto her block. She lived in the middle of the block with my Uncle Al, and their young adult children, Norman and Ethel.

When I went there for lunch, Aunt Bess was usually the only one home. She would make things for me to eat that my mother told her I liked – peanut butter and jelly, ham, various soups and the like. I always had a good time visiting with Aunt

Bess. She became my favorite aunt. Of course, she was the one I saw the most as a small child. So it was just natural for me to feel that way.

After visiting with Aunt Bess, I would wend my home and settle down to playing or a nap. The naps became fewer as time went by. My mother would always ask me what I did there and what I had eaten for lunch. I always told her. One day I said that I had eaten a ham sandwich with lettuce on white bread. My mother got all excited and wondered how I had eaten a sandwich with lettuce, as I didn't like lettuce. I told her that Aunt Bess' lettuce tasted good and that hers was terrible.

She immediately called her Aunt Bess to inquire where she got her lettuce and what kind it was. Aunt Bess told her that it was Iceberg lettuce and was nothing special. My mother immediately went to our corner store, the one at the end of street opposite of the way to Aunt Bess. She bought a head of Iceberg lettuce for me. The next day she put some on a sandwich and gave it to me. It tasted terrible, so I spit it out. I told her and took the lettuce off of the sandwich, which I finished eating.

That afternoon she went to see Aunt Bess to find out where she bought *her* lettuce and made her go with her to that store. We all went to the grocery store at the opposite of her block from the direction of our house. My mother asked her which specific head of lettuce she should choose. Aunt Bess, in a muttering annoyed tone of voice said, "Here, take this one," as she grabbed a random head of lettuce and handed it to her. My mother bought the head of lettuce, brought it home and the very next day made me another sandwich using it.

Once again, the sandwich tasted terrible with the lettuce in it and I spit it out. Once again, I told my mother and took the lettuce out of the sandwich. My mother was dumbfounded. I

guess there was just something special about eating lettuce in a
sandwich made by Aunt Bess at her home. No one has ever
understood the anomaly, including me. Aunt Bess' lettuce just
tasted good.

Cowboy

On one of trips home from lunch at Aunt Bess' home in 1949
at age 4 ½, a man with a pony stopped to talk with me. He
asked if I wanted my picture taken on his horse. I told him I
wasn't supposed to talk to strangers. He assured me that it was
OK to talk with him. I, being a trusting naive soul, continued
to talk with him. He convinced me to have my picture taken as
a cowboy sitting on his horse. He assured me that I was under
no obligation for anything. What did I know? It all seemed
harmless enough.

He proceeded to dress me up as a cowboy, put me atop his
Shetland pony and take my picture. He asked me my name and
address, which I wasn't supposed to give him, but I did. Don't
ask. I don't know why.

Several days later he showed up at our front door and showed
my mother the picture. She was furious. I had neglected to
relate the incident to her. Was she ever angry! I hid behind the
wall to the next room peeking around the corner to watch.

He then sold my mom on the idea of buying the picture of her
precious little boy all dressed up like a cowboy and sitting on a
Shetland pony. She bought the picture. How could she resist?
After all, it was her son – her pride and joy.

Later, still angry with me over the incident, I was sternly
reminded not to talk to strangers and that I should have never
let this happen. I wasn't punished, as I had expected. Rather

just left alone. But, the man got to sell the picture and make a living.

...dressed me up as a cowboy and took my picture...

Uncle Marty's Pickup Truck

My mother's brother, Uncle Marty, his wife, Aunt Dolly, and
their two sons, Sidney and George, came one afternoon in a
green pickup truck. Uncle Marty was one of the few people to
own a truck after the Second World War. He was an antiques
dealer and used it to transport furniture and antiques from place
to place. He was considered very fortunate because he had a
vehicle.

After a short visit, we all piled into the truck. My parents,
Uncle Marty and Aunt Dolly sat squeezed into the seat of the
truck. Sidney, George and I climbed in the open rear of the
truck. I don't remember where Ed was or if he even came. He
would have been quite small and probably was with a baby
sitter. Off we went to Chinatown in Philly for Chinese food for
dinner. It was a great time riding in the back of the pickup
truck with the wind blowing and the truck bouncing up and
down. With today's seat belt and other laws, my Uncle would
probably be arrested if we did this now. Of course, there were
hardly any cars on the streets then.

We arrived at the restaurant in Chinatown and climbed out of
the truck. Away we went for dinner. This was my first
adventure out of our neighborhood and my first time eating
Chinese food. It was a great time. The strange food and trying
to use chopsticks was quite intriguing. I wasn't able to master
the use of chopsticks during that escapade so I resorted to
conventional flatware – a fork and spoon. For some reason,
knives weren't provided in Chinese restaurants. The new
flavors were great and I ate and ate like everyone else. We,
like many still do today, shared all of the entrees so we could
delight in the various dishes that were ordered.

After dinner we walked around for a short while and then got
into the truck and journeyed back to our home in southwest

Philly. The ride was, once again, grand and we talked and bounced our way back. We were dropped off and my aunt, uncle and cousins went on their way to their home. I was tired and went straight to bed.

Vacuum Cleaner

For years my mother cleaned our house using a hand sweeper. It had brushes on rollers that turned as you pushed it back and forth across the carpet. It worked, but didn't always pick up everything. My mother complained every time she had to bend over to pick up something the sweeper didn't get. Emptying the sweeper was a mess, too. Dust and dirt always flew around while dumping the contents of the chambers into the trash making more dirt and more work.

One day a strange man came to our house with a vacuum cleaner that worked on electricity. It was quite common in those days for salesmen to come door-to-door selling their wares, e.g., Fuller Brush, encyclopedias, etc. What a great invention. He brought it in and showed my mother how to use it and how easy it was to empty. You just took out the filled paper bag and put in a new one. The bag was sealed with a glue-backed seal and went into the trash. No fuss. No muss. No dirt and debris flying all over the place. It was a canister type vacuum with a long hose and metal tubing. You could even use the exhaust side of the machine to blow air instead of sucking it. It came with all kinds of attachments including a paint sprayer with a glass jar to put paint in. My father actually used it several time to spray paint!

My mother loved her new vacuum. It made her work easier and did a better job than the old hand sweeper, and it took much less time.

When my mother used the cleaner on weekends when my father was home, he would play tricks on her by disconnecting the hose from the cleaner so there was no vacuum. It would take her a few moments to realize that it wasn't picking up anything and turn around to see what happened. She would give my father funny looks when he did this.

My brother's playpen was in the middle of the living room blocking part of the floor to be cleaned. This didn't seem to be a problem because the long shiny tube and head of the cleaner twisted and the carpet under the playpen could be cleaned easily by pushing it under the playpen.

Months later when we ran out of the glue-backed stickers that had a skull and crossbones with the words "Death" and "Disease" printed on them, my mother just tossed the bag into the trash. I got very upset because she didn't put the sticker on the bag and the trash men might get sick or worse – die. Finally new stickers came in the mail and she used them once more. However, when they ran out, that was the end of stickers on the bags. My father explained to me that it was no big deal and that far worse things were put into the trash without harming anyone.

Uncle Norman's Girlfriend

My mother's other brother, Uncle Norman, was still in the Army even though the war had ended some time ago. He would come a couple of times a month to visit and have dinner with us. He came in uniform and was a Military Policeman. He was not on duty, so he didn't have an MP brassard or leather and wasn't carrying a weapon. He was just Uncle Norman.

Whenever he came, my mother had a special white glazed coffee mug that he used for drinking. For many years he had some kind of condition and had to use this special cup so as not to contaminate anyone else. I never quite understood because he used utensils and dishes shared by everyone else. That's just the way it was.

One day, he came with a beautiful young lady. They sat on the sofa in the living room and talked with my parents at great length. They stayed for dinner and I was sent up to bed so I have no clue about much else that evening.

They came together from then on several times a month. I remember that I wanted to put my arm around her, but I was too small. Once when I tried, it got stuck between her back and the back of the sofa. I didn't mind. It felt good and was a nice feeling. I don't think she ever knew.

They later got married and the beautiful young lady became my Aunt Jean. I went to the wedding in the synagogue with the big pillars out front in Strawberry Mansion (section of Philadelphia). It was a big lavish wedding and I got in line three or four times to kiss the bride. I didn't understand that the reception line was to congratulate the bride and groom. I didn't know you were supposed to move on and let others congratulate them too. I just liked kissing the bride and did it as much as I could. No one, not even the bride, seemed to mind. After all, I was just a child.

Kindergarten

It was the fall of 1949. Because my birthday would be in January of 1950, I fell into the age group to start kindergarten in the September session of 1949. I was one of the younger children in the class at Harrington Elementary School. My mother made arrangements with the boy next door to walk me to and from school. He was paid a pittance to take care of me. Although he was older, he was still in elementary school.

My mother instilled in me the knowledge of my name, address and phone number. To this day I know that address and telephone number. This was just in case I got lost going to or from school or anywhere else for that matter.

It started out all innocent and fine with my neighbor taking me to and from school. I only went a half-day for the morning session. A full day, morning and afternoon sessions, didn't start until first grade. He walked with just me in the beginning. After a week or so, I suppose he missed walking with his friends and hooked up with them on the way one morning. They took a route different from what my mother had shown me and told me I must take. They went on different streets and up driveways. Although they were parallel paths to the way I was suppose to go, it was unfamiliar to me. I followed behind the group of boys, who really didn't want anything to do with a small child. They were big boys and that was beneath them. Eventually we got to school and even on time. I learned about streets and driveways that I had never seen. The walk took about twenty minutes or so depending on which way I went. It, to me, was really no big deal.

Kindergarten class was not like it is today. We colored on paper, had milk and crackers, took naps and generally played with the toys in the room. The girls always wanted to play with the dollhouse and have one of us boys play with them and be the "father." I did this on occasion and learned and enjoyed the experience. Mostly I like to draw and color. Once in a while we made things out of modeling clay. Things like ashtrays and candleholders. Smoking was big back then. My mother was a smoker, going through two cartons of Camels a week! However, she never actually used any of my ashtrays.

At the end of class I was normally picked up by my neighbor and taken home. This day he never came. My kindergarten teacher was quite upset and concerned about how I would get home. She didn't want to go about her business, as I was her responsibility. I assured her that I really knew my way home and that I could do it without any problem. Reluctantly, she sent me on my way. I knew my way home and went without a snag. My mother was very upset at my coming home late and was quite worried. She was even more upset when I told her I came home by myself because my neighbor never showed. From then on I went to and from school on my own. I found out years later that in the beginning my mother followed me, hiding behind trees and utility poles, to make sure I was OK and didn't get lost. Once she felt comfortable that I knew my way, she stopped following me and left me on my own.

Raisins and Maggots

Now that I was a "big boy" and knew my way around the neighborhood, I was sent on an errand somewhat distant from my street. My mother had purchased a box of raisins at the nearby supermarket. Unfortunately, when she opened the box, the raisins were full of little white maggots crawling around in them. To me, it was interesting. To her, it was a disaster.

She sent me to the supermarket to exchange the box of raisins. The clerk, a young man, at the store took the box of raisins from me and opened the lid. Sure enough, he too, saw the maggots crawling around inside and made a grunting sound. He promptly provided me with a replacement box of raisins and I went on my way home.

My mother was so proud of me for doing this errand all by myself. Of course, I have no idea whether she followed me or not. But I was a hero for the time being for taking care of this little problem.

Strep Throat

Sometime toward the end of the second session of kindergarten in early 1950, I contracted a strep throat caused by the Streptococcus bacteria. I was very, very ill. I ran a fever so high that a special thermometer was obtained to measure my temperature of 108 degrees. Everyone thought I was going to die. My mother was telling all the family and friends to come see me because it might be the last time. Family and friends came to visit. They brought all kinds of gifts for me. It was great!

I was moved into my parent's room and put in their dark walnut four-poster bed. My father had to sleep in my bed or elsewhere, which I am sure did not make him too happy. My mother wanted to be near me in case anything happened during the night.

In the mean time, I was getting sixteen injections of Penicillin a week. My butt was sore from all the needles I got. I was bed ridden and not allowed to take the covers off. I was just allowed to stick my feet out from under them for short periods of time. I was only allowed out of bed to go to the bathroom. I don't remember bathing, but I am sure my mother washed me allover regularly. Cleanliness was at the top of the list of details.

The fever went on for over a week. Even the pediatrician attending me was concerned that there was something severely wrong. He actually called in another doctor to look at me to see if he could figure out why my fever was so high and lasting so long. The consulting doctor determined that I was having an allergic reaction to the penicillin, which should be discontinued. I was given the "wonder drug" that was the predecessor of penicillin, sulfa. However, this was a newer version that was considered the new miracle drug. It seemed to do the trick, but I was still quite weak and messed up. I will not go into graphic description of the all the other symptoms, as most people really don't need that much information.

During the time I was bedridden, I experienced what could be characterized as hallucinations. They were interesting to me at the time and still are. I could feel the spindly posts of the bed without actually touching them. They were both very thick and very thin simultaneously. For many years after my recovery, whenever I got sick with a fever, I would have this sensation. Along with what I call the "thick and thin" experience, I had the sensation of smell of what I call the "sick smell." There is no way for me to describe it, as there is no other odor like it. It is not a real odor, but a perceived odor. It is in my nose and to this day I still experience it when I am not feeling well. Just a couple of anomalies of being sick, I suppose.

I was laid up for about a month. During this time I had many adventures without ever getting out of bed. The one that stands out the most is my overhearing my mother having a visit from the truant officer. In my entire life, I am the only person I have ever known to be visited by a truant officer. He spent the better part of an hour talking with my mother downstairs in the living room. She assured him over and over again that I was upstairs in bed and really quite ill - at one point on the verge of dying. He indicated that it was his job to follow up on truant school students, especially ones that were as young as me.

In the mornings I listened to the radio. There was Don McNeil's Breakfast Club where Don would talk about different current topics and play music to get your day started. He had guests on that he interviewed. Sometimes he described himself marching around his breakfast table to keep some humor in the program.

There were *The Shadow* and *Green Hornet* adventures. Many people have only heard about these programs or listened to them on the Old Time Radio tapes you can buy in the store. I listened to them live when they first aired as radio plays. They were so much fun and my imagination just ran away with itself. Even the commercials were interesting, especially the ones about Blue Coal. TV was no longer available to me since it was downstairs in the living room and I was confined to the bedroom upstairs, so I had to imagine what things looked like or what was going on like in days gone by for the adults of the time.

One evening while I was sick in bed, I guess my parents wanted to go out. So they arranged with my next-door neighbor's son to baby-sit for me. For a while I could hear him and his friends downstairs in the living room horsing around and making a lot of noise. Then the noise and commotion moved outside to the front of the house. Following that there was a lot of banging and rattling of the front door. They had locked themselves out! In a fit of desperation they went into the other next-door neighbor's house, the one common to our house by means of the roof over the front porch. They climbed out their bedroom window, went across the roof, opened the bedroom window in my parents room where I was and climbed back into the house. I never saw them any more that night, but I am sure they made sure not to lock themselves out again.

One of the many games I played to pass time while ill was with marbles. I made deep creases in the blanket like from a mountaintop down to the foothills and rolled the marbles down the crevices into one another. The first one rolled down and back and forth until it stopped. Each successive one hit the end one and came to a complete stop. The marble at the other end acquired all of the energy and moved away. Sometimes it rolled back into the next to last marble and caused the same effect on the first marble. I spent hours playing marbles. I learned about physics without even knowing I was learning about physics.

One of my out of town visitors brought me a Jon Gnagy *Learn to Draw* drawing kit. It had all kinds of drawing implements and a sketchpad. I learned to draw and made everything in the book by following the instructions. It made it so easy. I drew the dog, the covered bridge, the cartoons and many, many more things. I was so proud of my artistic abilities.

My grandmother, my father's mother, brought me some Little Golden Books with pictures and writing just for children. I particularly liked the book about transportation with the drawing of the stewardess and flying wing airplane. The books were nice. I read the page over and over again imagining what it would be like to fly in such an airplane.

After I recovered I had to take these very large yellow pills that contained iron. I was anemic and had to have iron supplements to get my strength back. I hated those pills. They hurt when I swallowed them and I was not allowed to break them up. They had to be taken whole. Why? I don't know. But whole they stayed all the way down with the pain that followed every time I took one. Eventually, I refused to take any more and just stopped. I still hate them even when I think about them now!

Finally, I was allowed to go back to kindergarten. Many of the children remembered me and asked why I was out so long. I remember standing on top of a ledge against a chain link fence in the schoolyard during recess and telling about my illness. A few children were truly interested. Most didn't understand or care. They just went about playing.

At the end of the school year I was promoted to first grade. School was out for the summer. In September, when I returned for first grade, we were given a long test to take. I am not sure why they thought we could all read since we weren't taught reading in kindergarten, but apparently we all could. I took the test and forgot all about it. I learned to write my name and began to read about Dick and Jane.

Ironing and Peek-a-Boo Clouds

My mother set up her ironing board in the dining room next to
the doorway to the kitchen, laid out the laundry consisting of
all shirts for pressing, filled up an old quart soda bottle with
water and pushed the stopper with holes in it into the opening
at the end of the neck of the bottle. She sprinkled water all
over each shirt, folded them up and then rolled them up. All
this while the iron was heating up. After a few minutes, she
unrolled the first shirt and began pressing out all the wrinkles
in it.

I was playing and running around the dining room table, and in
and out of the kitchen. It was a bright sunny day outside, but
too cold to go out to play. I watched my mother as she hung
the ironed shirts on hangers and carefully placed them to hang
so they wouldn't get wrinkled again. The clouds were moving
by at a fast pace outside causing it to alternate from dim and
bright. I told my mother that the clouds were playing peek-a-
boo with us. She just laughed and agreed. Life was good.

17th Street

After only a couple of weeks in the first grade at Harrington,
we moved from Southwest Philly to the West Oak Lane section
of Philadelphia. I remember being in my parents' bedroom in
the front of the house when the deed to the property came. My
father remarked about how many tax stamps were pasted on the
deed and that they all were cancelled to prove that the real
estate transfer taxes had been paid. This procedure of putting
stamps on things has long since been discontinued. My parents
were so proud to have a new home with a new deed.

All of the furniture that came with us was used by my parents
to furnish their new home. However, it was clear from the
beginning that a new dining room suite (we pronounced it

sweet) was in order. Not long after we moved in, my parents bought a completely new dining room set. It was all cherry mahogany and consisted of a table with three leaves, a buffet, a server, a china closet and eight chairs. The vinyl-covered telephone booth that went in the corner by the arch to the living room was one of two things that didn't match. It was bright red with black speckles in it to tone down the color. The other was the Philco console radio. The room was filled to the brim with furniture!

My father sat at the dining room table at the first of each month writing checks to pay the bills. One time he forgot that the table was real wood and signed a check after placing it directly on the table. The indentation of his signature was there for as long as I can remember. He was so angry with himself for doing such a stupid thing. This prompted the ordering of cushions or pads for the table including the three leaves that were stored in the back of the dining room closet. This would never happen again!

1st Grade

Within a couple of days I was registered at Rowen Elementary School and was off for my first day at my new school. My mother walked me from our house straight up 17th Street to the end at Northwood Cemetery where it met Haines Street. We turned left and walked down along the cemetery wall to the school at the end of the cemetery. My mother told me that I had to go this way to get to school, so that was the way I went. Unbeknownst to me, my mother followed me for several days to make sure I didn't get lost. She hid, once again, behind trees and utility poles.

I was welcomed to my new class by my teacher and introduced to the class. I was shown how to write my name on special wide-lined paper and learned, once more, about Dick and Jane.

We had milk and crackers in the afternoon like in kindergarten, but no nap.

After several days in my new school, the school counselor came and took me out of class. We went to another room, her office, which had different sized furniture in it. I was asked to sit down at the small table in a small chair like we had in kindergarten. She gave me a booklet that was an examination I was to take. She told me to answer all the questions I could in the time I was allowed.

I started to take the test and, after a few questions, realized it was the same test I had taken at Harrington before we moved. I told her this and she became upset. I wasn't supposed to take the same test twice. Apparently my records from Harrington had not arrived and she would look into it. I was returned to my first grade class to continue work with the rest of the children.

No sooner had I returned than an alarm sounded. It was a series of buzzing-like sounds that I did not recognize. The teacher announced that we were having a retention drill. I had no idea what that was. We were lined up and walked downstairs to the basement of the building with all of the other people in the school. It was explained that this was a drill to teach us how and where to go in the event of a real air raid or atom bomb explosion. We just sat there on the concrete floor on the side away from the windows. Boring. After a few minutes another sound came over the public address system and we all went back to class.

So began my days at my new school.

Along Came Janice

For months my mother talked about a new baby. Just like with Ed, she told me I was going to have a new baby brother or sister. She told me that my grandmother was coming to take care of me because she had to go into the hospital for a while. I was so excited. I was going to have new baby brother or sister. Wow!

Time passed, my grandmother arrived and my mother disappeared. A day or two went by. I went off each day to first grade class coming home each day, as usual, for lunch. Then my grandmother told me I had a baby sister, Janice. I got excited all over again. I had a new sister. I couldn't wait for her to come home. Grandmom told me which day she was coming home. I counted the few days over and over again.

I was in school. It was finally the day my sister was coming home. I was so excited that at afternoon recess I was all mixed up. I thought it was time to go home. My new baby sister Janice was home already and I needed to go home. I left the schoolyard and couldn't understand why I was the only one. There were no safeties to help you cross the street. Everyone was staying in the schoolyard. I went on my way home. My new sister was coming and I just had to see her.

I arrived at home and my grandmother asked what I was doing home so early. I told her that I needed to see my new sister and asked where she was. She told me that she hadn't come home yet and that I had left school too early. She wanted to know where my schoolbag and things were. Apparently in my excitement and anticipation over the coming of my sister, I left during afternoon recess and left everything at school. I didn't care. My baby sister was coming.

My grandmother called the school to let them know what had happened and that I was home safe and sound. She didn't want them to worry about me going missing and not returning from recess.

The rest of the afternoon dragged on so slowly. My anticipation had caused me to speed up and the world around me to slow down. Finally, my mother arrived with my new baby sister who were brought home by my father. Wow, my sister was finally here! All my mother wanted to know was why I was home so early. I explained all over again. I didn't care. My sister was here.

Singing in the Rain

It was Spring once more. I still didn't know many children in the neighborhood or on my street. So I kept pretty much to myself. A neighbor a few doors up called my mother to invite me to a birthday party for her son. They were going to the movies and then return to have a party with cake and ice cream and games.

I went to the party with a gift my mother gave me to give to the birthday boy. There were a lot of children there. Many, including the birthday boy, were about my age. It was just grand. I was introduced to everyone and began learning their names. Some lived on the street where I lived, others were family or neighbors from different places. After the introductions, we were gathered together and ushered into cars to go to the movie. We drove to the Broad and Olney area and went into the Bromley Theater. I had no idea where I was, so I stayed close to the birthday boy and the crowd of children I came with. The movie theater was full of children, as it was a Saturday afternoon. It was very noisy with people running and going every which way.

We were all taken to the candy counter to buy candy or popcorn to eat during the picture show. The movie had already started. It was *Singing in the Rain*. I didn't get to see the beginning so I didn't know what it was about.

No sooner had I gotten my candy and turned around, everyone from the group I came with was gone. They just up and disappeared. I looked and looked, but they were nowhere to be found. I watched Gene Kelly on screen as he sang and danced his classic dance in the rain. It was an intriguing scene particularly because I had no idea what it was about. But the singing and dancing were great. I kept wondering where all the water came from and where it went. The young engineer in me was in full swing.

Still unable to find anyone, I began to panic. I looked and looked over and over again. There was no one I knew. I didn't know what to do. The Burl Ives song from my phonograph record kept going around and around in my head. "Remember your name and address, and telephone number, too. And, if some day you lose your way, you'll know just what to do. Walk up to that kind policeman, the very first one you meet. And, simply say, I've lost my way and cannot find my street."

I left the movie theater and went out onto the sidewalk where there were people everywhere. I was scared and crying. I saw a policeman and went towards him. He seemed preoccupied with something and I became even more frightened. I stood on the street corner crying. A car pulled up and a woman rolled down the window on the passenger side of the car while leaning over from her seat behind the steering wheel. She began to talk to me and asked what was the matter. I told her I was lost and couldn't find anyone I was with.

She told me to get in to the car and she would take me home. Abandoning all teaching about strangers, I got into the car. I told her my address and we were off riding around. She tried to find my house, but kept getting mixed up. She said, "Oh, N-o-r-t-h Seventeenth Street," making me think we were on South Seventeenth Street at one point. We were not, but what did I know.

Finally, we arrived at my house. I was relieved and happy to see my mother. The lady told my mother what happened and my mother thanked her for bringing me home. Of course, now came the lecture once more. I shouldn't have left the movie theater. I should have done this or that. I listened and did not reply.

After a while, my mother talked with the birthday boy's mother and assured her that everything was all right. The woman was really upset at losing me. I was sent back to the party for cake and ice cream and told to apologize for what I did. I did and had a grand time.

The now classic movie, *Singing in the Rain*, is one of my favorite pictures and always brings back memories of that adventure.

Playing with Matches

I was home for lunch between the morning and afternoon school sessions. I ate lunch while watching *Lunch with Uncle Pete*, a popular local lunchtime TV show of the time. Then it was off to school again. I got dressed in my winter coat and donned my hat, which I hated. I didn't like hats. They messed up my hair. Mom said I had to wear it, so I did.

It was a cold afternoon. The clouds were rolling around in the sky and the wind was blowing mildly causing the fallen leaves to rustle along the ground. They swooped up into tiny whirlwind circles and spun around and around up against the sides of the houses. The leaves crunched under foot. Some people were collecting and burning the leaves. What a wonderful aroma. Others just raked them in a pile and wet them to keep them in place until the city trucks came to collect them.

While walking to school, I came across a pack of matches lying on the sidewalk. I wasn't supposed to have or play with matches. So this was an exciting event. A whole pack of 20 paper matches in a complete package. They were the kind that came with packs of cigarettes from a vending machine. They were plain and unmarked except for the required marking of "CLOSE COVER BEFORE STRIKING" printed above the strip of flint-like material for striking the match to ignite it. What a great find, or so I thought. I picked up the pack of matches and put them in my coat pocket to check out later. I continued on my way to school. It was uneventful, after that, to say the least.

I arrived at school; lined up in the schoolyard; and went to class. Time passed and it was recess. We all got dressed to go out into the schoolyard for afternoon recess, which generally lasted about twenty minutes from start to finish. This meant we had about fifteen minutes outside not counting the time to lineup once more to come back inside.

Now was my chance to check out the book of matches I found earlier and put in my coat pocket. I found a place near the school building by a fence along the steps down to the Girl's Room and took out my find. I bent over to work on the ground lighting a match. I tore it from the book and struck it across the flint-like strip to light it. Nothing happened. I did it again. Again, nothing happened. I tried a different match. Nothing. Apparently the matches had gotten wet and were no longer functional. Bummer! And then, a teacher, the speech therapist with the Boston accent who tried to teach Philadelphia children to speak like Bostononians, grabbed me and told me to stand against the fence. I was being reported for playing with matches. Ugh! I stood there in disgrace while all the other children lined up and went back into class. I was brought to her room and made to wait while she told her class what I had done. Finally, I was returned to my first grade classroom and allowed to continue with the day's work.

I knew I was in trouble, but had no idea how much or what kind. I didn't think much more about it. Unbelievably, nothing happened! I got away without any punishment. How could this be? But, it was.

When I got home that day, neither of my parents made mention of the incident. I thought sure the school would have notified my parents. They did not. No one knew what had happened.

Several days later in the week I was with my mother visiting at my Aunt Pearl's home down the street. Uncle Dave's sister, Fanny, was there with her son, Jay. While we were all talking, Jay, whose teacher was the one who caught me playing with matches in the schoolyard, related the encounter to everyone. I was found out and my mother was appalled. I was reprimanded on the spot and punished even more when I got home. I was grounded for a week - a whole week! I was not allowed outside to play for the weekend and rest of the following week. I was restricted to being in the house and not allowed to play with any friends or have company. It was boring most of the time.

Did I learn anything? Nothing I didn't already know. Don't play with matches. It's not safe. Don't play with matches in the schoolyard. Don't play with matches in the schoolyard where the entire population of the school can see you. Was I stupid, or what?

The Berkshire Mountains

It was my great fortune to grow up in an era when the vast majority of things were assembled using fasteners that could be undone. Most things were put together with nuts and bolts and were readily and easily disassembled. Many an hour was spent taking apart electrical parts – turn switches, toggle switches, lamp sockets and fixtures – as well as many other things. As a budding engineer, I had to know how things worked. So, I reverse engineered everything I could get my hands on. I took apart old locks and learned how pin tumbler and skeleton key locks work. I opened up old light bulbs and learned how the wires were placed to allow the glowing filament to create light without damaging things internally and externally. I liked to wire things together. Soon I became an expert at making wires carry electricity to do things.

At the end of my first grade came summer. My grandparents on my father's side decided to take a trip to New England's Berkshire Mountains staying at their children's homes along the way. I was 6 ½ years old and excited about my very first trip. My mother packed my clothes and necessities in a single suitcase and sent me off on an adventure of a lifetime!

Grandma Gussie and Grandpa Harry picked me up and off we went to New England. Our first stop traveling along the parkways of Pennsylvania, New Jersey and New York states was a gas station on the side of the parkway in New York just before the Connecticut border. The service attendant filled up the car with gas, checked the oil and water while Grandma and I went to the bathroom. While I was still outside the service station building a ways from the car, my grandfather drove away with my grandmother. Grandma told Grandpa that I was not in the car. He assured her that everything was fine. He was just moving the car to the side of the station away from the gasoline pumps. I was lost and just stood petrified at being left behind. Then Grandma appeared, explained what happened and ushered me back into the car to continue the trip North.

We arrived in New Haven, Connecticut at the home of my Aunt Rose and Uncle Raymond. Cousins Marlene and Muriel greeted us exuberantly along with their parents. It was nearing dinnertime, so we unloaded the car quickly and got ready for dinner.

After dinner, we sat around and talked for a while. We children mostly listened. Then, it was time for bed. We were all sent upstairs to wash and dress for bed. I no sooner got changed into my pajamas and went to the bathroom door when it flung open and out came Marlene and Muriel stark naked! I was dumbfounded. I had never seen girls undressed before, except for my infant baby sister, Janice, a long time before. They giggled and ran off to their room to dress and go to bed. I did my bathroom things and went to bed, too.

We only stayed the night and were off again in the morning moving further into New England. We traveled on to Massachusetts where we stopped to visit with Aunt Stella, Uncle Mac and Cousin Billy. Again, we arrived around dinnertime and the same evening rituals proceeded. I slept in the same room as Billy. He went to sleep quickly in a new and strange position. He lay on his side with his arms folded out in front of himself and stayed that way most of the night. I tried to go to sleep the same way, but found it uncomfortable.

The next morning Billy and I went out in front of their home and played for a while. Billy had found some cigarette butts and a pack of matches. We were going to build a small fire with them. We piled the cigarette butts together after shredding them. Billy struck a match and began to light the little pile of stuff. It just smoldered and went out. He tried again. The same thing happened again. After several tries, we abandoned the idea not knowing that cigarette tobacco wasn't supposed to catch fire. We ran around and played some more.

Once again, it was time to push on. The car was loaded up with the luggage and ourselves and we began our journey north once again.

As a child, I thought we were in New Hampshire, but later I learned we were still in Massachusetts. We arrived at an old farmhouse after traveling along country roads with no sidewalks – a novelty to me being a city boy. Aunt Jean, Uncle Bode, and Cousins Paul and Flip greeted us on our arrival. Again, it was late in the day and we settled in for the long stay. This was our destination and abode for the next week or so.

I took my suitcase to a back bedroom that had bunk beds. I was to sleep in the upper bunk closest to the ceiling. So close that I was unable to sit up in bed without hitting the ceiling. I unpacked my things and placed them in dresser drawer out of sight.

During my stay, we went swimming, fishing, mountain climbing and all sorts of other things I had never done before. I caught my first fish – a Perch. I took it back to the house, cleaned it and gave to Aunt Jean to prepare and cook. I ate that fish that evening for dinner. Yum!

One morning I found Grandpa and Uncle Bode out in the barn trying to repair a light socket with a pull-chain. I watched eagerly as they tried over and over again to get it to work. After a little while, I spoke up and told them that they were doing it wrong. They looked at one another and then looked at me. Uncle Bode said that he wasn't able to make it work and that maybe I could.

I was unable to reach the light socket, which was way up high. Uncle Bode was on the ladder and I told him how to reposition the chain through the hole in a direction opposite to the way they had it. He put on the shell covering, screwed in a bulb and, voila! The thing worked. I was so proud. They were so astounded. But it was done and we went on to do other things like boating and walking around in the woods.

After the week or so went by, we reversed our trip order with the commensurate stay over at each of my family's homes and returned home. My mother was happy to see me and asked me to tell her all about my vacation. Once again, she was so proud of me when I related the story about the light socket.

The Front Door

Toward the end of that summer, my parents (more likely, my mother) decided to have a new front door lockset installed. A man came and took the old lockset out and spent a lot of time working on putting in the new one. He was very meticulous about his work and kept the place clean.

All the while he worked, my mother and I sat on the studio couch in the sun parlor watching him. I learned a lot more about locks and how they worked. We sat there for some time and then he began doing basically the same things over and over again. He was unable to get the dead bolt to function properly. He would take off the deadbolt knob and cover plate, make some adjustments to the mechanism and replace the cover plate. Then he tested the deadbolt. Over and over again only the key or the deadbolt knob would work, but never both together properly. He tried again and again.

In watching the man work and carefully observing the mechanism, I had deduced the error of the assembly. I spoke up and told him that I knew how to make it work. He looked at my mother. My mother looked at him. He said that since he wasn't getting it, that he was willing to try what I would tell him. I told him to remove the deadbolt knob and cover and to set a particular part of the mechanism a certain way. He followed my suggestion. I told him to put the cover back on and try it. It worked. And, once again, my mother was so proud!

The Bicycle

For my birthday, one of the many presents I received was a bicycle. It was a red, 26 inch Schwinn bicycle. It had a coaster brake and no gears. It was one of many to become a classic much later. One of the other presents I received were bike accessories from Aunt Pearl and Uncle Dave. They gave me a leopard-like seat cover with a foam rubber cushion, real foxtails that went into the holes in the handgrips and a bell that clamped on the handle bar. It made my bicycle really neat. Most of the children who had a bike owned one that was old and beat up. Only a few had a relatively new bike to ride.

It was the year that Elizabeth was crowned Queen of England. It was an age of electronics and television. Two of the major networks had a race to get film of the coronation back New York City and show it on television. The audio could be sent over the Transatlantic Cable, but video was a whole other story. There were no satellites and the cable couldn't carry video. So a scheme was devised to take motion pictures using movie film and develop the film on airplanes while enroute from England to the United States. It was a massive undertaking on the part of the two networks.

I watched the coronation on TV early in the morning when they only transmitted the sound and showed still photographs of what was happening. The pictures had been taken earlier and were reasonably accurate. They talked about how the horses were trained not to respond to the noise of the crowd. They had them pull the royal carriage through the streets early in the morning while making loud noises by clashing metal trash can lids and other implements so the horses became accustomed to the racket and wouldn't bolt with the queen in the carriage. It was all very interesting. Hours after the real coronation was finished, the film arrived in New York City and was shown on TV. One network was a few minutes behind the other with almost identical movies of the happenings. It was a wonderful time. Everyone looked terrific all dressed up in their finest togs for the event. Queen Elizabeth was just beautiful. Every little boy's dream girl, I suppose.

I rode around the neighborhood fantasizing that I was pulling the queen in her carriage with my bicycle. I had *some* imagination. I had a grand time. I started out along one street, stopped for a while pretending she waved to the crowd and then moved on. It was a great time and I had a lot of fun.

Later, during the summer, I took my bike to the schoolyard to play. I was so proud of my bicycle with its foxtails and seat cushion. I parked near the gate by the end of the cemetery and went in to play. Several hours later when I returned to go home for lunch, I found that my bicycle had been vandalized. The foam cushion was gone from under the seat and so were the foxtails. I was very upset. Who would do such a thing to my nice bike? I cried all the way home and told my mother about what had happened. She said not to take it to the schoolyard any more. I never took it again. I agonized for a long time over the loss.

Hebrew School

Several weeks after the start of fourth grade I must have gone through some rite of passage. What it was, I will never know. Probably just being old enough. I was told that I was going to start Hebrew School after school on Tuesdays and Thursdays with an additional class on Sunday mornings. Being Jewish it was time to get a formal education in the history, religion, ethics and culture of my heritage. So began my religious training with more rules and morals that one can imagine. Like most religions, it came with a lot of baggage that I was expected to carry. So I carried it, but, with many questions.

We belonged to and I attended Ezrath Israel at 69th & Ozontz Avenues in West Oak Lane. Regular school ended at 3:30 p.m. in the afternoon and Hebrew School went from 4:00 to 6:00 p.m. Afterwards, the long walk home for dinner. The synagogue was even further in a direction away from my home than was school. Dinner was usually around 7:00 p.m. Then homework. Then bed. I hated Tuesdays and Thursdays for a long while.

My first challenge and major question came on my first day of Sunday school. Having been indoctrinated in my first two sessions during the week, I was now an old hand at finding my way around the synagogue and Hebrew School. But, when we started to read Genesis in the Torah (in English, of course), I found it very questionable that Cain kills Able then goes off to the city to marry a wife. Where did this city come from if Adam and Eve were the first people and Cain and Able were their only children. How does a city suddenly pop up from nowhere? A city, let alone just other people in a small area!

I was confused to say the least. I raised my hand (I was not and am still not bashful) and asked about this. The explanation I got was the standard answer about it just being an explanation of things back then. It still bothers me to this day. I love to think about it as one of the anomalies in the Bible. Although bible scholars have an explanation for this, I still struggle with it. (Please don't write me about this. It has been dragged around for too long now.)

I went to Sabbath services. Children's services, which were, for all intents and purposes, pretty much the same as the adult services, but with 50-75 noisy children. I learned my religion as most second generation American Jews do, just what I needed to know. Just what they wanted me to know. I went to Hebrew school through the age of fifteen. Most children considered becoming a Bar or Bat Mitzvah their ticket out. I didn't see it that way. For me, it was a way to learn.

The other anomaly was that we did not practice in our home what was taught in religious classes. My mother had been soured by an experience when she was young and chose not to practice the religion. My father and mother had never lived in a kosher home, so no hint of kashreth (keeping kosher) existed outside of the synagogue.

Printing

Somewhere along the way I was given a rubber stamp printing kit. It had moveable rubber type that could be set in a stamp holder to create a custom rubber stamp. There was only one holder, but lots of type – letters, numbers, and punctuation. I made up business cards and calling cards for my self and family members. I even sold a few sets of cards to neighbors. It took a long time to assemble a stamp. Then I had to cut up paper into the size of a business card and stamp the cards after pressing the stamp on the inkpad. The most difficult part was getting the printing on the card straight. I did everything by hand. There was no mechanical means to align the printing on the card. It was all done by eye.

One day I was walking along Old York Road and came across a printing company that had everything needed to do real printing. I went in and told them what I was doing. I think they felt sorry for me rather than ever consider me competition. I obtained real properly cut business cards that they made up for me using a guillotine to cut the paper stock square. I was in heaven. Square business cards that were the correct thickness.

I reprinted one order for one customer and gave it to her for no additional charge, as I didn't think the work I had done initially was very good. She was very pleased. I think she was just being nice to begin with by buying my work. She was a neighbor two doors down from us.

Later, when I went into junior high school, I had shop and was able to further my knowledge and abilities by working in the print shop with real type made of lead. I learned to set hot type. I learned how to lock the type in a frame and set up a printing press. Of course, all of the old forms of typesetting are obsolete now, having been replaced with computers, composing and word processing software, and other printing methods.

The Tent

At some point my parents replaced the Venetian blinds in some rooms in the house and put the old ones in the basement for safekeeping. As time went by, they were disassembled and only the wooden slats and top mounting remained. We made games out of the top parts, setting them up so that when we rolled marbles down the center slot, the marble would go from slot to slot and roll all the way down to the floor. We called it shooty shoots. We spent hours on end playing with the marbles and configuring the wood with the slots in different ways.

One day during the summer, I figured out how to use the slats to enlarge a tent I made. I had strung a clothesline between two clothesline poles in our driveway and draped an old quilt over it in the form of a tent. I used rocks from the broken up driveway to hold down the sides. Tent pegs were out of the question in concrete. Then, I had a brilliant idea. I put the slats from the old Venetian blinds across the inside of the top of the tent and held them in place with clothes pins clamped over the quilt and slat. It made the tent wider and voluminous. It was great.

Some of the neighborhood children came along and began pulling the clothespins off to make the tent collapse. I chased them away. One boy kept coming back and messing up my tent. I told him that if he didn't keep away he would be sorry.

Back he came, over and over again. Finally I had had enough. I chased him all over the driveway without catching him. I picked up a rock from the driveway and threw it at him. I was never able to pitch very well and was amazed when it struck him dead center on his right side seriously hurting him. He began to cry and ran to his grandmother's house very much afraid of me. Unfortunately for me, his grandmother was our neighbor two doors down. She was the one who had purchased the calling cards from me.

I later learned that I actually fractured his pelvis. What a pitch! I didn't mean to break any of his bones. I just wanted him to stop messing up my tent and leave me alone. And, he did.

Cub Scouts

A schoolmate of mine talked me into going to a Cub Scout meeting to see if I was interested in joining. I finally agreed and we met after dinner on a school night. We met at the end of 17th Street at Haines along the cemetery wall. We walked to the home where the meeting was being held on 19th Street around the corner on the other side of our elementary school.

My friend and I went into the house and downstairs to a finished recreation room where other Cub Scouts were gathered. Suddenly a boy yelled out that he didn't want me there. Lo and behold, it was the boy whose bone I broke with the rock. He was very upset. I was in *his* house! I was upset, too. I wanted to participate in the Scout meeting and learn what is was all about. It looked like I was out.

His mother, who was also the Den Mother, talked with him and explained that this is what the Scouts was all about - getting along and learning. She talked him out of wanting me to leave and made me welcome in her home. I was allowed to join and participate in all the activities. The boy I injured settled down and we eventually became friends again.

At a later meeting in another person's home, I was shown a machine that the father used. He was in the cigarette business and had vending machines in various stores and restaurants. The machine put from one to four pennies in between the plastic wrapper and the paper packaging of a pack of cigarettes. This enabled the machine to take your quarter and return your change in the package. (Yes, cigarettes were cheap back then!) Sometimes I was more interested in watching the boy whose house we met in run the machine than the Cub Scout meeting itself. All in all, I had a grand time in Cub Scouts and later the Boy Scouts.

First Came The Wind

First came the wind followed by rain. It came like a moving waterfall from the next driveway between the rows of houses in the city. The schoolteacher living next door cried out, "Here it comes. You better get inside." This meant only one thing, another boring summer afternoon inside the house with nothing to do but putter around in the basement.

We lived in a row home on a street where there were approximately 30 houses on each side. Our home had a stone front facade. Brickwork was everywhere else except for the poured concrete foundation. A window-glass shop occupied the garage. In the basement was an oil-fired boiler, a huge red horizontal cylinder with jet-black bands that looked like Santa Claus lying down. A make-pretend space ship communications system that I made was wired up in the bead board bathroom stall. It connected to another control panel alongside a workbench separated from the rest of the basement by a wood frame partition. We used it to take imaginary trips into space and back again. The lights were wired in such a way that when a light was turned on in one location, it was also turned on in the other and vice versa.

A dual 48-inch fluorescent lamp fixture, suspended from the ceiling, illuminated the workbench. Being the victim of having the fluorescent tubes smash on me, I had placed two bands of black electrical tape around it to keep the fluorescent tubes from falling down when someone banged on the floor above to get someone's attention. On the workbench sat my father's machinist's tool chest of drawers from his time working as a sheet metal shear operator. It contained precision tools – a micrometer, calipers, scales, scribes, wrenches, gauges and much, much more.

Behind the workbench area was a 275-gallon heating oil tank painted a muted silver color. Strange sounds would come from it when banged depending how much oil remained. Most of the time it made a low, echoing, hollow sound. Next to it stood an old grey filing cabinet, which could be locked, but seldom was. The key just stayed in the lock. It was filled with all sorts of papers and stuff.

In another area was a small bench with a chemistry set and glassware all set up. More on this later. At the back end of basement, near the stairway leading up into the house, against the wall that was the back of the garage, was a desk and small office area where the business part of the window-glass operation was conducted. Opposite were the washer, dryer and a double washtub at the piping and pump end of the boiler. A small short corridor led to the back door along the other garage wall.

The concrete floor was partially covered with an old piece of linoleum. The uncovered ceiling was just crossed braced open rafters. It had knob and tube electrical wiring connected to the porcelain light fixtures powering 100-watt incandescent bulbs. The unfinished walls were the plain concrete of the foundation with red brick and off-white mortar starting at the top for the party walls on each side of the house. The front of the basement had two windows high up that looked onto the patio and shrubs above ground in the front of the house.

An American Flyer model train layout that I designed and built occupied the central part of the room. It had an inner and outer oval of track connected at one end with switches. A small village was incorporated as part of the layout. Totally automated, the locomotive and train on the inner track waited for the locomotive and train on the outer track to clear the switches. Then the switches automatically threw to set the inner oval complete. The inner train then roared around, stopping once again at the semaphore as the switches returned to their original position allowing the outer train to complete its run. The electrical wiring powering the tracks, switches, signals and building lighting were all strung on the miniature utility poles as part of the layout. Once started, it was a self operating system. A wonderful sight with the basement lights turned off.

An intercom, which I acquired from my father's boss and installed, sat on a shelf over the workbench housed in a makeshift wooden box. It was connected to every room in the house and could "listen" to everything going on all over the place as well as communicate with each room. It was connected to the telephone line so that conversations could be monitored or conducted. Eavesdropping? Of course!

Tools, electrical stuff, papers, books, and toys. You name it; it was there for the asking. What a wonderful place to be bored.

Outside, the rain continued. But strange and magical things were happening. The cloud ended about a foot from the backs of the houses across the driveway. It was dry and warm beyond the cloudburst end. A small model airplane engine could be heard to whine and stop, and whine again, interspersed with laughter and shrieks of joy. Children were outside on this rainy day, playing at the rain's edge. Dancing around. In and out of it. Teasing it. Daring it to come closer. It never did. It wouldn't dare!

The Driveway

For many years the common driveway in the back of our house was in a state of disrepair. There were several large areas where the concrete paving was gone or broken up with patches of dirt and gravel. We called the gravel by a name that was more like its look – potato stones. The smooth, round gravel stones were called potato stones because they resembled little skinned and washed potatoes. The ruts, stones and irregular concrete made for a playground of adventure. With toy cars and trains, the terrain made a wonderful make pretend land of adventure for endless imagination.

In the warm weather, we played various games in the holes filled with potato stones: construction, road races with our miniature toy cars and trucks, rearranging the stones to make imaginary pictures or buildings and so on. When it rained, we made little streams forcing the water to go this way or that. In winter, when the water became slush, we splashed it around with the potato stones or made slush balls to throw, but not at each other. When there was ice, we ran and slid standing up on it. We seldom fell. And, amazingly, no one ever was hurt!

The driveway was a playground for us. We rode our bikes, rode our wagons, roller skated, played ball and many other outdoor games suited to the small "T" shaped area. Many of the houses had clothes poles to hang clothesline on for drying laundry. Very few had or used electric or gas dryers. Even Mom hung clothes out on warm days instead of using our dryer. When we played, we were very much aware of these poles and avoided them without incident. We were also aware of the holes. We rode our bikes and wagons through the holes to experience the bumps from the potato stones.

Spring came and there was turmoil. The City of Philadelphia sent a letter to every house on the three sides of our driveway informing the property owners that they were being assessed for repair of the driveway. Many complained bitterly about the cost, especially those who had houses where the driveway was not in a state of disrepair. Others simply just couldn't afford it. Not paying the assessment was the same as not paying your taxes and would be handled in the same way as a tax lien - foreclosure and sale of your house out from under you! People were hopping mad.

Everyone survived the commotion and eventually forked out the money. The construction began. Heavy equipment moved into the driveway and began tearing up all the concrete of the driveway. Many people, like my dad, paid a separate, additional fee to have the short driveway from the main one to our garage repaved. The potato stones were gone!

During the construction period we figured out that heavy equipment had no requisite key for starting up the engine. Whenever the men saw children watching when they were starting up or shutting down the equipment, they would try to hide what they were doing. It only helped us figure out where to look for the ignition. A few of us played on the equipment after the men left. Some of us actually got it started! When we did, we were scared out of our wits, as we didn't really expect it to start. Then came the problem of how to shut it off. No one dared try to make the equipment work or move. That would be a catastrophe!

The cement mixers came and poured cement into the driveway and men shaped the concrete with long boards and long cloths that were dragged down each poured section to create the surface texture for traction by the automobile tires. Finally, the driveway was done and we could play there again, but it was never the same.

Towards the end of the construction of the new driveway, Mom, being the frugal person she was, saw an advertisement for children's shoes at our local Buster Brown shoe store. Unconditionally guaranteed for one full year! Mom ran with us to the store and bought us each a pair of the "unconditionally guaranteed" shoes. The next week my brother Ed took the wagon to the top of the new driveway, which ran downhill, and proceeded to ride the wagon down the driveway. It was a lot of fun. All of us had done it at one time or another. But this time was different. Ed dragged his brand new shoes while going downhill in the wagon. Not only did he drag them, he dragged them on the tops of the toes of the shoes. Within a short time they were scraped all the way through to his exposed socks on both shoes! Mom was furious. Off she ran to the Buster Brown store with Ed and exacted a replacement pair under the "unconditional guarantee." She had already had words with Ed about what he could and could not do with his shoes. Back he went in the wagon rolling down the hill. Feet in the wagon this time, he stopped by using the sole and heel of the shoe with minimal dragging, when he got to the bottom. The shoes lasted a lot longer this time – a whole year until he outgrew them!

After The Rain

Around nine o'clock the rain was gone. In minutes the ground was dry. Children began coming out to play their street games. It was much better now that the center driveway was completely repaved. Now the concrete was new and made way for different venues. A small baseball diamond was painted half way down its modest slope for half-ball games; a bottle top court on a side driveway to a garage; a hopscotch court on another.   There was plenty of room to chalk up works of art and games. There was a basketball hoop attached to the shed of the back of our house overhanging the door to the garage and glass shop.

Between some side driveways were small patches of ground where grass or shrubs grew. In winter, snow forts abounded there. Behind the glass shop garage were snowball bushes (hydrangea) colored pink and purple. Games of tag were played around these obstacles. Sometimes in them, to the dismay of some. Scientific talk, school talk and philosophical talk about days, even years and decades to come were engaged there.

It was an era when laundry was hung out to dry even if you had one of those new gas-fired clothes dryers. Strung on clothesline between the four poles planted at the corners of the side driveways and propped up with longer wooden poles specially made for the job of lifting the sagging lines. Clean, bright laundry blowing in the gentle summer breezes made for soft, wonderful smelling clothes and bed sheets.

Sometimes, when no one was playing in the center drive, red Radio Flyer wagons and all sorts of bicycles were coasted down the incline to make a breeze to cool hot bodies. One of the other garages up the driveway was used as a storehouse and workshop for gumball machines. Cases upon cases of gumballs, chewing gum packages, candy and gumball prizes were processed there. You didn't need to win a speckled, striped or other strange gumball when purchasing gum to get a prize. The people who worked there were happy to give you any of the prizes for free! Prizes, such as King Tut in a sarcophagus, Chinese finger locks, twisted wire puzzles, tiny decks of cards and the like. One of the "older" boys who worked there would show off by performing acrobatics for entertainment.

Only a few automobiles populated the side drives. Many were kept inside their respective garages. Many more were parked on the street in front of the houses. Weekends would see cars being washed. Soapsuds running down the center of the driveway to the main street at the bottom. They continued on and down the storm drain at the street corner by the orange fireplug, which was in front of the dentist office.

Dinnertime arrived. We went through the back door into the basement and up the stairs with the overhead pantry shelving into the kitchen. The kitchen was a typical row home kitchen for West Oak Lane. There were two windows in the kitchen. One over the gas stove on the back wall. And, one in the nook on the side wall. In the nook was a totally unique fire engine red vinyl covered booth from Mickey's luncheonette! It fit perfectly into the indentation of the sidewall under the offset window. Mom used the space in the bottom to store pots and pans. Chachkes hung on the walls above it. It had a refrigerator, sink, stove, cabinets and counters and a Formica topped kitchen table. The table was against the booth in the nook and had four vinyl covered, stainless steel tubular chairs – one at each end and two in the center opposite the booth. The usual kitchen cabinets hung above and below on the opposite party wall. The refrigerator was an older Coldspot from Sears, Roebuck and Co. that never needed repair. Between the sink and the nook was the doorway to the shed that hung over the driveway to the garage underneath. Its door was only closed during the cold months, as there was no heat in the shed. The linoleum covered floor served to promote stocking footed sliding across the kitchen floor from a running start way off in the sun parlor at the front of the house. The routinely accumulated cooking grease on the nondescript Sanitas ceiling was ready for cleaning. On the top of the booth by the window lay a grey metal grille covered loudspeaker connected to the intercom on the shelf above the workbench in the basement. Wide wooden Venetian blinds covered the double hung, wood frame windows, which were kept open during the warm months. On the outside of all of the windows were aluminum storm windows with screens typical of the 1950s, used during the warm months.

Washing the Car

It was a warm summer afternoon in 1955. The trees were plush and the flowers in full bloom. Walking down the front steps of my home on my way to the schoolyard to play, the trees rustled in the breeze. I looked down the street, which was a somewhat steep hill, and saw Uncle Dave. He and his wife, my mother's sister, Aunt Pearl, lived about a quarter way up from the bottom of 17th Street. We lived half way up the street. He was washing his brand new 1955 Chevrolet - his pride and joy. He meticulously washed and rinsed the car. Carefully wiping it dry.

Suddenly, I could not believe my eyes! Uncle Dave was now inside the car washing the inside of the car. He had taken the hose into the car and was washing everything with the water squirting from the hose. The inside of the roof; the seats; the dashboard; the upholstery. You name it and it was being washed! The water was now running out over the door thresholds into the street. What a sight to see!

I didn't wait to see how he got the water out. I just went on my way. Laughing, laughing, laughing. As I recall, the car never was the same. The stench was there forever! But… it ran. And, it ran well, much to everyone's surprise.

On the Way to the Schoolyard

As I continued on my way to the schoolyard, I walked along the streets and driveways of the row houses in the West Oak Lane section of Philadelphia. Philadelphia, being about 35 miles across, had many sections. Each one unique in its own way. We lived in West Oak Lane, west of East Oak Lane, north of Olney, south of Mt. Airy and so on. West Oak Lane is larger than most small towns in the United States. The route I took to get to the schoolyard could have been any one of a half dozen ways to go. Philly streets, alleys and driveways are laid out in a rectangular grid in keeping with the plan of William Penn, its founder. Of course, there are exceptions, such as Ogontz Avenue, Germantown Avenue, Cutler Street, and many more too numerous to mention, that go on an angle to the grid or just meander through the city.

The hucksters were wandering up and down the driveways, those areas where motor vehicles went in between the backs of the row homes to gain access to the garage under the house from the rear. They were selling fruit and vegetables fresh picked early that morning, knife sharpening services, fresh eggs and a multitude of other things. It was a time when most women didn't work; drive; or even own a car. They were home during the day and had their windows open to keep the house cool – few had air conditioning then – and would listen with anticipation for the calls of the men selling their wares and services. "San Hart Jersey tomatoes." "Free stone Alberta peaches." "Fresh picked watermelon; cantaloupe." "Knives sharpened!" Once in a while an organ grinder with a monkey came and played music. As mentioned earlier, a man with a

Shetland pony would dress you up as a cowboy or cowgirl and take your picture on the pony.

At the top of the hill bounding all the named and numbered streets in our neighborhood was Haines Street, the southern border of Northwood Cemetery. It was long, straight and had a paved sidewalk that ran the length of the cemetery and the school – William Rowen Elementary School, where I was headed. The school was named after a Civil War general whose portrait hung in the main entranceway of the school, the place where none of us children were allowed to go except on very, very special occasions. On the side of the school was a plaque constructed as part of the building that read, "Education is not a mere means to life. Education is life." It was not attributed to anyone. Not even the word anonymous was there. However, it is known to be the words of William Rowen, the very person the school is named after!

At the Schoolyard

When I reached the schoolyard, the gates were unlocked and open. The schoolyard, now a summer day camp, was teeming with children. None of us were able to attend a real day camp, so we came here, or were sent here so our mothers could have some time (peace and quiet) without us. There were innumerable activities all conducted by a single man in charge of the playground adapted from the school and its yard. There were arts and crafts, baseball, basketball, volleyball, tether ball, hop scotch and bottle tops played on the painted courts near the school building, tag and catch around the big tree in the side of the yard, and contests with prizes. My particularly favorite prize was Fleer's Double Bubble Gum!

There were no facilities available on the outside of the school building. The two water fountains were off. The boys and girls rooms were locked. Permission from the man in charge was required to use the facilities inside. Even though one door was unlocked, no one was allowed to enter the school building without permission and no one did.

On rainy days we were all ushered into the school building and sent downstairs into the basement gymnasium where indoor activities were conducted. There were mostly arts and crafts, like wood burning, watercolor painting, colored construction paper activities, and molding and painting using plaster of Paris.

Today was contest day! I couldn't wait to continue working on my project that would be judged later that afternoon. I arrived and immediately got out my project. I set it out and sat down to work on one of the many brown-painted Shaker-style benches. I was making a hat. Not an ordinary hat. A hat to out do all other hats. It was a multi-level, extremely embellished object of art. Or, so I thought at the time. It started out like stove pipe hat and then continued with several tiers of exaggerated topping after topping. It had rings made into chains that were draped from its every side. All this from colored construction paper. What a hat it would become!

The afternoon lingered on. It was warm and sunny. A gentle breeze blew often and would cool the air for a few moments as the temperature rose into the high 80's. The clouds played peek-a-boo for a while and then just bright sunshine for the rest of the afternoon. Everywhere there were children. Some working on their entries for the contest. Others just making things, running or playing games.

Being pre-occupied with my illustrious work of art, there wasn't time to do much else. I was busy carefully cutting out calculated pieces of construction paper and pasting them together. I used the kind of white paste for school children that came in glass jars with a stick applicator mounted in the center of the screw-on lid. I doubt that it was non-toxic. It might have been, but no one knew or cared back then.

Several hours went by. My creation was done. It was wonderful! And, it even fit on my head and stayed there. Of course, I had to wear it for the contest. It was, after all, a hat! The man in charge announced it was time for the judging of the entries. He pulled out his long list of contestants who had registered for the contest and asked if there were any more people wanting to enter the contest. No one answered. Then, it happened. One by one, he took the prizes out of a large cardboard box. There is it was. The first prize. An entire box of Fleer's Double Bubble Gum. The excitement in the group of children was electrifying. We all wanted to win the bubble gum!

Everyone present judged the entries much like the old time dance couples with the master of ceremonies holding his hand over each contestant's head and listening to how loud the applause and cheers were. One by one, the man in charge held his hand over each contestant's head. One by one the hand clapping and cheering rose and fell. It was my turn. To my astonishment, the applause was louder and the cheering greater than anyone before or after. I was astounded. I couldn't believe my hat was actually liked by so many. After all, it was just some colored construction paper thing I dreamed up. But it was judged the best. I had won the box of Fleer's Double Bubble Gum. That delicious pink bubble gum with its unique flavor and sweetness. I won! I won! I won! Wow!

Working with Dad

The days passed slowly to the weekend. Sometimes you like the time to go by more quickly. But, when you are on summer vacation from school, you really like when it goes slow. The summer seems to last longer that way.

It was Saturday. Dad had already prepared for Saturday's
work of installing window glass on the construction site of new
homes. He spent several nights prior measuring and cutting
glass to size in his glass shop in the garage of our home. The
shop had everything a modern, up to date shop should have. It
had a cutting table covered with carpet to keep the glass being
cut from getting scratched. It had wooden crates of different
sizes of glass. Some of these weighed a 100 pounds or more.
There were various custom made mirrors ready for installation;
all kinds of specialized tools and things for the work:
glasscutters, special shaped pliers, wooden rulers (yard sticks)
and putty knives. There were special papers to place between
sheets or lites of glass so they didn't scratch one another.
Chinese markers to mark the glass for cutting. Putty, linseed
oil to soften the putty, solvents, cloths and rags for wiping and
cleaning, and scrap buckets for the breakage or broken glass.
Knives, hammers and saws. There was wood molding to hold
the glass in the windows. This was used to replace molding
broken during removal of a broken windowpane.

Dad worked full time as a salesman for H. L. Bennett Glass
and Mirrors. He got the job years earlier. When we came
home from our summer vacation down the shore in Wildwood,
NJ one year, the sheet metal company where Dad worked had
closed. He was out of a job. He got in touch with his father,
who sold glass and mirrors. He was hired immediately to do
the same. Now four generations of Goldmans were glazers:
my father, his father, and my father's father before him, all the
way back to England, and now me!

The only story I ever heard about the glass business in England
was that a horse drawn wagon carrying several panes of glass
was on its way making a delivery. A strong wind came, lifted
a lite of glass off the wagon and blew it down the street. It
landed, crashing to the ground and shattering all over the place.

Then there was the family joke. A double entendre on the words pain and pane foisted upon me to no end. All of my growing up years adults, particularly my grandmother (my father's mother), would say to me, "Your father may be a glazer, but you are a pain!" This would happen when I would be doing something or be somewhere inconvenient for the grownups. My brother and sister encountered this less frequently as they were both younger and less often in the way.

The green '55 Ford station wagon had been loaded the night before and was ready to go. We got up, washed, dressed and headed off to the job site. Along the way we stopped at a Dunkin' Donuts shop for coffee and donuts for breakfast. The coffee was fresh made, as were the donuts. A "dunkin' donut" was one that was basically a cruller with a small piece added on for a handle to hold while dunking it in your coffee. Yum!

We arrived at the job site. Hundreds of houses were in various states of construction. We got right to work installing and replacing window glass. It was hard work carefully removing the window moldings so as not to break them. The broken glass, glazing points that held the glass in place and the insulating putty all had to be removed. Then the new glass was put in. Sometimes additional custom glass cutting was required because the window frames made in the mill were not always square or straight. My father or I would free cut the glass by hand to make it fit. Then the new glazing points were installed. Sometimes by hand, but most times with a hand gun that put them in perfect every time. Putty was put in the frame muttons for insulation and to keep the glass from rattling. Then we would put the molding back in place being careful not to break the pane of glass again.

When the broken windows, if any, in a house were fixed, we went on to hang a mirror in the bathroom. Many times the order to install the mirror came too soon after the plasterers were done plastering the walls. Hanging a mirror on a wall that was not fully dried caused the lime in the plaster to leech through the mirror backing. This turned the silver into spots of silver oxide rendering the mirror full of black spots. My father kept warning the builder about this. But it often fell on deaf ears. Then, like now, project timelines mattered more than quality. Get the house completed so settlement was on time and the people could move in. The black spotted mirror would be dealt with later during the warranty period.

The mirrors were hung using "J" hooks as seats at the bottom. Adhesive backed cork was placed inside the hooks to keep the mirror from being scratched or chipped. Rosettes were used at the top to hold it to the wall. The protection of the back of a mirror is more important than the front. The coatings on the back are softer than the glass front. If the back is scratched, it appears in the mirror and is not repairable, requiring replacement.

When I first started working with Dad, I was the gopher. Go for this. Go for that. Now I was still the gopher, but did actual work and was being paid, to boot. Wow, money!

Gunshots

A loud gunshot resounded from the next house. Then another. And, two more. Dad said it was the electrician. He was doing installations and used a .22 cal gun to put studs in the concrete walls of the houses. I continued on and finished the tasks at hand wondering all the while how it was actually done. Wouldn't the object the shell was shooting crack the concrete wall? Wouldn't there be a ricochet? Why use a gun and not a drill? Was it a gun like in the movies? It was all very new and intriguing. It heightened my curiosity. The gunshots stopped for a while and then four more resounded later, further away. Apparently the electrician was in another house.

Dad was finishing up one of several window replacements in the house we were in. As my curiosity was getting the best of me, I asked if I could go see what the electrician was doing. Dad said OK. I hurried to find the electrician. I didn't want to miss seeing what he was doing.

I found the electrician several houses away getting ready to shoot some more. I ask him and he explained what he was doing and how the gun worked. I watched with amazement as he shot four studs into the concrete foundation of the house without so much as a scratch or crack anywhere. He then proceeded to mount the electric meter box onto the four studs and, using nuts for the studs, tightened the box into place on the foundation. Then he connected the wires to the terminals in the box. Neat as can be!

He showed me a .22 cal blank cartridge – no bullet. One of the ones he used to fire the gun. He explained about the safety mechanism on the gun. How it couldn't fire if it was not pressed against the wall disengaging a safety mechanism. The studs were specially made hardened steel to withstand the force used to penetrate the concrete wall and stay in the wall.

When he wasn't looking, I tucked the cartridge into a pocket in my dungarees. (They weren't called jeans yet!) But, he was too sharp for me. He said that I shouldn't have taken the cartridge without asking and that it was very dangerous. I gave it back to him, but he declined, saying it was OK for me to have it as long as I understood what it was and could do. Whew!

We talked for a while longer while he worked. I figured I had stayed long enough and better get back to work with Dad. I thanked him for the cartridge and for the time he spent teaching me about his work. I went on my way, back to the house where Dad was working.

Lunchtime

Sometimes we would see my Uncle Dave and his crew. Uncle Dave was a painter and paperhanger. He had several men working for him painting the interiors and exteriors of the houses. They used brushes, that new invention, the roller, or a sprayer for unfinished basements and they sprayed everything: the walls, the floors, the ceilings, and the windows. You name it, they painted it. It was easier to spray everything and then go back and clean off the window glass.

Painting with a roller caused a lot of controversy. The union and non-union painters alike didn't want the roller because it would allow more work in less time. Therefore, less wages overall with a shortened job duration. Management, like my uncle, saw it as a boon to get more work and complete it faster. I never did understand why there was such a to do over the roller, when spraying was even quicker. History shows the roller won out.

It was now lunchtime. Dad and I packed up the station wagon and headed for the nearby tavern for lunch. It was located up on the main road about a ten-minute ride from the jobsite. When we arrived, we entered through screen door before the front door that was open. It was dark inside. My eyes had to adjust to the dim light. Inside there was a straight bar with a dark mahogany finish backed up to a wall behind the counter where the bartender would move up and down waiting on the patrons. It had booths to sit in along the opposite wall. There were the usual bar signs all lit up. Some in the windows facing out to the street. Others inside advertising the various beers and liquors available for consumption.

I was allowed in, but not allowed to drink alcoholic beverages, of course. Dad liked to have a draft beer with lunch. I would always have birch beer. It was delicious. We usually took about an hour to eat our lunch and socialize with the people there.

Dad enjoyed the interaction with the other people at the bar and the bartender. There were some Saturday regulars like us. There were other workmen from the jobsite. I just liked the idea of being there, where I was normally not allowed by myself. Sometimes I ate roast beef. Other times, a plain Philly steak sandwich – no cheese. The food was good and the surroundings enjoyable.

When we were finished eating, Dad would pay the check and always leave a good tip for the bartender. I learned that when you frequent an establishment on a regular basis, the service is always better when you tip a bit extra. You set an expectation for the next time you come in and it is generally fulfilled.

It was back to work. There were another three hours or so left to finish replacing windows and hanging mirrors. Since we started early in the morning arriving on the job around 7:00 a.m., we would finish around mid-afternoon. It was a long day, but the summer days were long and there would be plenty of daylight hours left to do other things after returning home and unloading the station wagon.

Saturday Evening

Dad went into the sun parlor, laid down on the studio couch and took a nap. The sun parlor was a room that had a large opening to it from the living room. The sun parlor was narrower than the rest of the house as there was a large opening between our house and our neighbor's when you came up the front steps. The front door was on the side facing the mirrored house and had windows with large slatted Venetian blinds. The party wall had a large framed picture on it. There were two chairs with a tiered table between in addition to the studio couch. Under the side window in the sun parlor was a hot water radiator with a radiator cover over it. Dad kept his magazines there – US News and World Report and the likes of that – most boring stuff to me at the time! The floor was carpeted wall-to-wall and continued throughout the living room, dining room, up the stairs and throughout the upstairs hallway. We knew about the hardwood floors underneath, but wall-to-wall carpet was the fashion of the day.

In the living room, was our Dumont television housed in a cherry mahogany cabinet with doors that swung open to either side enabling viewing of the picture. It had a green "eye" for tuning in stations correctly. This TV didn't have a detent tuner to change channels – one that clicked when turned. It was continuous and required that the "eye" be set. In those days there were still only three channels in Philadelphia. WPTZ Channel 3, WFIL Channel 6 and WCAU Channel 10. It was the golden age of television. But we didn't know it then! TV shows were mostly live and not on 24 hours a day. They only aired in the morning, afternoon and in the evening until 10:00 o'clock. Then the stations would sign off the air by playing the Star Spangled Banner, our national anthem, and either power off leaving snow for a picture with noise and static for sound or transmit an Indian Head test pattern with a continuous tone. There was no late night TV. You either found other things to do or went to bed. Of course, young children went to bed at 7:00 p.m. Older ones, depending on age, either 8:00, 8:30 or 9:00. Mom and Dad went to bed at 10:00 p.m.!

On either side of the TV were wing-backed chairs. Those who watch Antiques Roadshow would love to have any of the furniture we had. Except the TV, of course! Atop the TV was a lamp Mom had made from a large glazed and kiln fired figurine. It had a rectangular fringed lampshade that curved down and out from top to bottom. Facing the TV on the opposite party wall was a sofa with a real down cushion centered between two leather topped end tables with shaded lamps. The wall facing the street, which was alongside the opening to the sun parlor, had a window with the same closed Venetian blinds as in the sun parlor. We didn't want anything to fade from the sun, so the blinds were nearly always closed when the sun was out. Under the window was another radiator with cover. Next to the window was Mom's throne – a large, cushiony chair covered in suede-like material where she sat many an hour smoking Camel cigarettes and reading paperback dime novels.

By the stairway going upstairs, was a 3-tier table with chachkes (knickknacks). The stairs used to make a 90-degree turn coming down and had a small landing at the turn. Many years earlier, Mom had a carpenter straighten out the steps to make more room in the living room. This extra room is where the tier table sat with an electric torch lamp alongside. The torch lamp had a 3-way bulb that could be turned on at 50, 100 or 150 watts.

Hanging over the mantle was a large brass reproduction charger with an Old-English tavern scene embossed in it.

Opposite the stairs on the other side of the opening to the dining room was a fireplace set at a 45-degree angle in the corner. It had a mantl with more chachkes on it. The area above the mantle was wood with a large frame outlining the area. Hanging over the mantle was a large brass reproduction charger with an Old-English tavern scene embossed in it. In the fireplace were two andirons and a lighted electric log. The log had two slowly turning discs that simulated a flickering fire. As the fireplace was originally designed for gas, it did not have a chimney. It was cool looking just the same. We took photographs in front of it as it made a great backdrop.

The next room was the dining room. It had a traditional cherry mahogany dining set. A table that took three leaves and was covered with custom made pads. Arranged clockwise around the dining room table against each wall were a buffet, a china closet and a server. There were two armchairs and six side chairs. There was a door to a coat closet that was under the steps to upstairs and over the steps to the basement. It was a rather large closet having a series of shelves with lots of things stored there and was full of coats. It was one of our hiding places when playing hide-n-seek or just hiding from Mom when we were in trouble. A vinyl-covered telephone booth (yes, just like those pictures of 1950's things) sat between the coat closet door on the wall behind the tiered table in the living room by the stairs. On the wall opposite the phone booth on the other side of the opening to the living room was a dark wood console Philco radio. Above the radio hung the door chime for the front and back doors. It would make a ding-dong sound for the front door and a dong sound for the basement backdoor.

To the left of the china closet, facing the back of the house, was a window covered by a Venetian blind. To the right was the kitchen doorway. When we first moved in it had a door that swung either way. But, Dad took it down because he and Mom thought it was inconvenient and would make the rooms look and feel bigger. Above the dining room table was a crystal chandelier with large clear candelabra type light bulbs. On the server were two hurricane lamps. I never understood the term, as they were electrified and useless in a storm if the power failed. I guess it was more a description of the style of lamp rather than its function.

Mom was in the kitchen preparing dinner. Being Saturday, it was cold cuts night. She was setting out cold cuts – salami, bologna, rolled beef and corned beef. There was Jewish rye bread, cole slaw, potato salad, mustard, pickles and sour tomatoes. From the basement storage area came 8 oz. bottles of Sweetie Beverages flavored soda – root beer, lemon-lime, orange - and plain seltzer. There was a bottle of beer and a Pilsner glass for Dad.

Dinner was ready and Mom called us in to eat. My brother Ed and sister Janice sat in the booth. Dad at the head of the table. Mom sat on the side between the table and the sink so she could get things easily and I sat at the end opposite Dad.

While we were eating, Dad would tell about the events of the day from his perspective. The rest of us contributed some to the conversation, but mostly ate. Janice was at an age where she wanted to drink Dad's beer. For weeks she had been asking to have some. Finally, Dad gave in thinking she would take one sip and not like it. He handed her the full glass of beer and turned to Mom to talk. When he turned back, it was all that he could do to get the glass of beer away from Janice. She had just about finished the entire glass of beer. Much to Dad's surprise, she loved it!

After dinner, each of us children was required to take turns cleaning up the kitchen. Tonight was my turn. I hated it, but did it nonetheless. After the leftovers were put away and the table cleared and wiped, it was time to wash the dishes. It took me so long to wash the dishes that the hot water always ran out. Consider that there were no pots and pans this evening; it was amazing that it still ran out. I suppose I was too slow and took too much time listening to the kitchen radio.

The three of us children all went outside to play. It was still
light out and all the neighborhood children were out and about
playing Philadelphia street games. We played hide-n-seek,
Baby in the Air, wire ball, half ball (stick ball), flipped cards,
follow-the-arrow, hopscotch or bottle tops. Sometimes we
would catch lightning bugs (fireflies, glow worms).
Sometimes we would just talk. We never knew what we were
going to do as we made it up as went. There were no home
computers or Internet and no one had an interest in TV. There
were board games, but it was still light out and we had to be
out. We had great fun in spite of ourselves and the times.
After all, that was what we knew and we loved it!

We stayed out until after it was dark. Generally 'til around
9:30 or 10:00 o'clock. Times being what they were, no one
worried about getting mugged or into trouble. Life was simple.
Life was grand. No cares. No worries. Just playful fun. One
by one we went home. Some were called by their parents.
Others just went home when their friends did. Off to bed!

Sunday Morning

When I came downstairs on Sunday morning, everyone was in
the kitchen. Ed and Janice were having cold cereal and milk.
Mom was drinking coffee and smoking a cigarette. Dad was
frying up salami and eggs in the old black iron frying pan. The
smell was just wonderful. The toaster was making crisp toast
to go with the salami and eggs. I got the box of Kellogg's
Corn Flakes, poured myself a bowl full and added cold milk.
Yum!

When I was finished eating, I went into the shed at the back of
the house through the door from the kitchen. It wasn't really a
shed. It was another small room with a door to the porch
between our house and the neighbor to our other side where the
schoolteacher lived. The shed had a jalousie window and was

really a cupboard with built in cabinets and drawers. It wasn't used to store food; there was no heating in the room and nothing under the floor on the outside. It was cold in winter and hot in summer.

I looked to see if the little bird I had found injured a couple of days ago was on the mend. It had died. I wrapped it up in some old cotton cloth and proceeded outside to the back of the house to bury it. I picked up a small toy shovel in the basement and made my way through the back door and out to the small patch of ground between the schoolteacher's house and ours.

It was an interesting patch of ground. Some of the houses on our side of the street had this type of ground in between the driveways of the houses and some were just paved over with concrete. Ours had the snowball bush, some other shrubbery and a small bit of grass and dirt. In the winter, when it snowed enough, we built a snow fort there using the snow Dad had shoveled when he cleared the driveway for the car. Now it would be a graveyard for the dead bird.

When I finished burying the bird, I went back inside and cleaned up in the basement sink. The idea of germs, disease and death had entered my head from all of the teachings of my mother and school. Scrub, scrub, scrub! When I figured I had washed enough, I dried my hands and arms and went upstairs to the first floor to see what everyone else was doing.

Mom was in the living room smoking a cigarette, drinking coffee and reading one of her dime novels. Dad was reading the Sunday paper. Ed and Janice were nowhere to be found. I located the comic section of the paper and settled down in the sun parlor to enjoy the funnies. It was a quiet time in the morning.

The Red Booth Incident

Dinnertime in our home came with mixed emotions from us children. We were hungry, of course. However, most of the time we did not look forward to the evening ritual. Mom made us eat all of our dinner. If we didn't eat all of the meal, we were not allowed to leave the table. We hated eating all of our dinner. Most times it was just too much food. Other times the food just didn't taste good. She insisted that everything served to us must be eaten. Yelling and screaming was a mainstay during dinner. It was the post WWII era and, after all, there were starving children in Europe! Many were the times that one of us would respond with, "So, send it to them."

Janice had devised a way of dealing with this problem. She simply and discreetly stuffed whatever food she didn't want to eat into the space between the seats of the booth into the bottom cavity under the seat where Mom stored her pots and pans. She always appeared to have eaten her entire meal. She always got to leave the dinner table first. It was an ingenious way of coping with the rules of dinner and it worked!

This way of reducing her food intake worked for some time. Then... Mom needed a special pot she did not normally use. She lifted up the seat of the booth to find it crawling with all sorts of bugs! They were crawling all over the inside of the booth bottom. You could here the screams for miles. They must have awoken the dead!

Mom spent hours cleaning out the booth. It had to be immaculately cleaned. This entailed removing every pot and pan stored under the all the seats. Dozens of things were removed, washed and dried. The booth was washed, disinfected and dried, too.

Needless to say, Janice got into a lot of trouble.

The Party

The next week slowly moved on. Bicycling, roller skating, street games, some indoor activities and more time at the schoolyard. Saturday was coming and that meant the monthly family gathering would be at our house. My mother's relatives were coming that evening to party, just adults, only aunts and uncles, no cousins. The dining room table had all three leaves in it and was covered with the custom padding and a pretty embroidered tablecloth. It was an after dinner gathering, so only light snacks and drinks were served.

Mom was in the kitchen preparing the food for the evening event. Bridge mix was her favorite to serve. It was easy to prepare. Open the bag and pour into serving bowls. There were pretzels, cookies and cakes. Dad put the drinks on the buffet on trays. There were the usual ice bucket, glasses, soda, and liquor.

The family began to arrive and the noise level began to rise. As more people arrived, more conversations ensued. They got louder and louder. Then Uncle Dave arrived and his voice could be heard above everyone else's. Uncle Dave was just plain loud when he got excited. The conversations spread out throughout the house all the way into the kitchen from the sun parlor. Finally, the men and women separated. All of the men sat down at the dining room table to play cards. Uncle Marty was the major card player of the family. He played pinochle and poker mostly. This would be a poker crowd so everyone could partake. And, they bet real money – no chips! The women gathered in the living room and began to gossip. Stories about different people the group knew who weren't there.

There had been a murder in the family. A niece of Aunt Pearl had been killed by her husband. No one ever said anything

about a motive. They just theorized about how it was done.
The husband was a butcher and, therefore, knew exactly where
her heart was when he stabbed her. Of course, this was all
conjecture based on the newspaper account and my aunt's
discussion with her sister in law, the murdered woman's
mother. The trial had not begun at this point, but he was
eventually convicted of first-degree murder and sent to prison
for life. Aunt Pearl was vague in most of her discussion even
though she thought she was the expert on the subject. She
provided a very authoritative account according to her.

The conversations moved on to other news and gossip items of
the day. After the murder account, no one conversation
dominated the women's talk. In the dining room, the men were
well into winning or losing at the poker game. Uncle Marty
was already half way through his cigar. He was hardly ever
without a cigar during these big games. Come to think of it, he
was seldom without a good cigar.

The evening moved on and it was time for the children to go to
bed. One by one we said our "Good night" to our aunts and
uncles and went upstairs to bed. Once in bed, the din of the
party downstairs seemed to go on forever. Uncle Dave's voice
still seemed to dominate the talking most of the time. Finally,
sleep came to us. The party eventually ended sometime in the
wee hours of the morning.

When we awoke Sunday morning, all traces of last night's big
party were nowhere to be found. Mom and Dad had cleaned
up and the house was back to normal.

Smedley Hill

Within a few minutes walk from the back of our house was
Smedley Hill. We walked up our driveway, turned right at the
"T" at the top, turned left onto Smedley Street and walked

across 67th Avenue to Smedley Hill, the congregation point for dozens of children. It was well suited as a play area because, although it was half of the bottom "T" of a driveway in the backs of the houses, the driveway itself was a steep slope of about 50 degrees. Automobiles were generally unable to traverse it. It was a paved area the depth of the houses about fifty to sixty feet wide. Only show off young drivers with cars having a short wheel base would ever attempt it lest they bottom out at the top or smash the front or back of the car at the bottom and get stuck there.

On any given day there would be children playing jump rope, hop scotch, tag, roller-skating, bicycle riding or just talking. Smedley Hill was an ideal area because there were no playgrounds in West Oak Lane except for the schoolyard almost a mile away. Those on bikes enjoyed the quick fast coast down the hill. You had to walk your bike up the hill or ride around the short block and up the gentler slope to get back to the top. Riding up the hill took great strength and was nearly impossible unless you had an English racer set to the lowest gear. Then, maybe, you had a chance.

Everyone was friendly and most knew one another from school or the neighborhood. Once in a while someone would bring an old broomstick and some pinky or pimple balls cut in half. We would use them to play stickball or half ball – a baseball-like game requiring a smaller playing field as the hitting distance of the ball was much shorter. The half ball didn't have enough energy to break anything. We used large stones or scratches on pavement for base markers. We never had an umpire. We just worked out the questionable plays by discussion or, sometimes, argument.

Hardly anyone ever got hurt even though the entire area was paved with concrete. Even then, the worst would be a scraped knee, hand or elbow. No big deal. You went home, got patched up and came back.

Smedley Hill was the "in" place to be. We didn't know it then, but it was. We had fun and passed the time playing. Our parents were happy, particularly our mothers, because we were out of the house. Basically, not around to give them grief!

Good Humor

Every day after dinner, while were going about our early evening activities or outside playing, we heard bells ringing as the Good Humor ice cream truck came around the corner and up the street. Summer ice cream from the Good Humor man was a treat. We would go running to Mom or Dad and ask for money to buy ice cream.

The truck would stop half way up the street and everyone lined up at the window in the side of the truck. The Good Humor man, a young lad trying to make a couple of dollars during the summer season, parked the truck and began waiting on his customers. The truck was covered with pictures of ice cream treats and had a menu next to the window where the driver served you. There were rockets (push up ice cream in a printed cardboard tube on a plastic stick), fudgecicles, creamsicles, chocolate covered ice cream bars, ice cream sandwiches, cones covered with chocolate and nuts, cups of vanilla and chocolate that came with a wooden spoon and a lid that had pictures of movie stars to collect, and various other forms of the sweet stuff.

I liked the rocket and the cone. When I got an ice cream cup, I would work on stirring it and waiting for it to soften. It became soft ice cream and was yummy. I ate it slowly so it would last. I used the spoon to scrape the cup and get that itty-bitty last bit of ice cream out. Yum!

We would congregate in the street or sidewalk or someone's patio and talk while we ate our treat. Then back to whatever game we were playing. The sun hadn't set yet so it was still quite light out. As the evening went on, it slowly got dark around 9:30 and lightning bugs would come out and flash their little lights like so many thousands of little twinkling stars under the trees.

The darkness, lit only by a single street light converted from an old gas lamp, made the street games we played more challenging as it was harder to see what we were doing. In particular, when we played a game with a ball, it was a real challenge to see the ball, catch it and keep track of where everybody was. We all had a grand time. It was good to stay up and out late without having to worry about school, homework or chores.

Having played hard all day, when it was time to go home to bed, we were tired and slept quite well. This pleased our parents.

End of Summer

It was coming up on the week before Labor Day. Time to start getting ready for our week down the shore – the Jersey shore. Every year our family spent a week in Wildwood, New Jersey at the Beachview Hotel. We stayed in a room in the basement of the hotel for a week where we had a private entrance to our efficiency. Mom liked it because it was the only room in the hotel where you were allowed to cook. Although, most of the time we ate cold cereal breakfasts and cold cuts lunches there, once in a while Mom would make a hot dinner on a hot plate. The rest of the time we ate out at various places on the boardwalk or a block or two off the boardwalk in town.

Each of us began getting things together to take down the shore. Most of the items were clothes, bathing suits, towels and washcloths, medicine cabinet stuff, comic books and other reading material, and beach towels, of course! Everything needed to sustain the comforts of home away from home.

Dad packed our green '55 Ford station wagon. Most of the suitcases went on the roof and were tied down. The back seat was put down flat so the rear area of the wagon had lots of room for us three kids to spread out a blanket and be able to play and nap in the back. There was plenty of room for us to horse around yet not be on top of each other. Seat belts wouldn't be on the scene for at least 5-7 years. Car seats for children would take much longer. We loved to bounce up and down when the car went over a bumpy stretch of road. It was like being on an amusement ride. And, of course, like all children, we had our fights. It was all Mom or Dad could do to separate us during these episodes. The back was fun to be in! It was the place to be on a long trip – ninety miles to the shore!

It was time to leave. The gas tank was filled, the oil checked, everything was ready to go. Mom had checked her ashtrays in the house to make sure they were all empty – no cigarettes burning. The thermostat for the heat was set to 55. The window blinds were all closed. All the doors and windows were locked. Janice, Ed and I were in the back of the wagon. Mom in passenger seat – she didn't have a driver's license and never drove. Dad was in the driver's seat. Off we went.

The drive took about two hours or so. We wound our way through the city towards the Tacony Palmyra Bridge. Near the bridge was a man selling Philadelphia soft pretzels. Dad pulled the car next to the curb and for twenty-five cents Mom purchased five soft pretzels for us to snack on. The ones that now sell for over a dollar each and aren't anywhere near as tasty!

Suddenly traffic stopped as we approached the bridge. The open girder semicircular span of the bridge was going up! A boat was navigating its way up the Delaware River through the open bridge. Fifteen minutes later, the bridge finally went down. After crossing the bridge, Dad paid a nickel to the toll collector in the tollbooth and we continued on our way.

We drove through the small Jersey towns on our way down the shore. The only limited access highway didn't come until we were almost to Atlantic City. As we got closer to the shore, we stopped at one of the roadside farm stands selling produce fresh picked that morning. Mom bought some fruits and vegetables for us to eat while we were away. It was cheaper than in the grocery store or supermarket back home.

We got on the Garden State Parkway and headed south towards Wildwood. It was a toll road. Every so often we went through a toll where Dad paid a nickel to continue on. One stretch of road had a parallel road without a toll. Dad took it and saved five cents! Five cents was a lot then.

As we neared Wildwood, Mom sighed and said, "Smell that salt air. Isn't it wonderful?" It was the smell of the inlet and always smelled bad to me, but Mom loved it. We finally arrived at the Beachview Hotel. Dad pulled the car into the parking lot near our basement room. He went around to the boardwalk entrance to check in while we began unloading the car and putting our things next to the door to the room.

Dad came back with the room key and let us in. We brought all of our things into the room and Mom set up for the week. The room was dark. The only window was next to the door and was under the porch for the rooms above, shaded from the sunlight. A small lamp lit the room. It had beds and a table where we would eat. We hurried to get things in order so we could get as much beach time in before evening.

Finally, we changed into our bathing suits and headed for the beach. We went out of our room, alongside the hotel, under the boardwalk and onto the sandy beach toward the ocean. At last we were on the beach. Mom set the blankets on the sand and opened up the beach chairs for herself and Dad. She gave us the usual lecture about safety and pointed out the landmarks of buildings back at the boardwalk so we knew where she and Dad were on the beach. We were off to the water – the ocean – the Atlantic Ocean. It was warm and relatively calm with waves breaking just a few dozen feet before the shore. Ed was like a fish in the water. No sooner was he in swimming, when the lifeguards were blowing their whistles for him to come back closer to shore. He was on his way to England! Annoyed that he couldn't stay far out in the ocean, he reluctantly came closer to shore.

Janice and I stayed closer in. I couldn't swim and Janice, being still quite young, wasn't allowed out far. We rode the waves, jumped and played for a long while. Mom came to get us saying we had had enough for now and had to go back and sit on the blanket. So, we went back and played in the sand using our buckets and shovels to build sand castles and the like. As I mentioned earlier, Dad, who, for medical reasons, wasn't allowed to go swimming or be exposed to the sun, was still dressed in his street clothes including white sox. I don't think he even owned a bathing suit. Mom had already mixed up her baby oil and iodine, which she used to coat her skin for that instant sun tan look. You couldn't have white skin if you were down the shore.

The sun had moved from overhead to over the buildings on the boardwalk. Evening was fast approaching and it was time to go back to the hotel room and get ready for dinner. We packed up all of our things and headed back. Once there, we each showered and dressed for the evening. Sand was everywhere even though we worked very hard at showering outside first to wash it all off. What would the shore be like without those annoying little grains of sand here, there and seemingly everywhere?

After we were all cleaned up and dressed, we went up onto the boardwalk, the raised platform of wood that went along the shoreline in front of the buildings for a couple of miles or so north to a couple of miles or so south. The Beachview Hotel was pretty much in the center of things. The stores, shops, arcades and restaurants were in full swing. There were literally thousands of people as far as the eye could see up and down the boardwalk. We went into a restaurant a short distance from the hotel and settled in for dinner. It was an American style restaurant – steaks, chops, seafood and the like were the fare on the menu. We ordered drinks, which were served first. I ordered hot tea with lemon. Mom and Dad had coffee; Ed a soft drink; and Janice a glass of milk. Unlike the time a few years earlier in Atlantic City at Shumsky's kosher restaurant when I ordered hot tea with lemon. I had no sooner squeezed some juice from the lemon when Janice added some cream and it all just curdled right then and there. Even though it was quite hot outside, the tea was good. I could feel it go all the way down to my stomach each time I took a swallow.

We ordered dinner and ate while trying to decide which way to walk on the boards – the boardwalk. And, eventually coming to the conclusion that the amusement rides Ed, Janice and I wanted to go on were south. So that's the way we would head. Dinner was good, but dessert was even better. I had a butterscotch sundae with banana ice cream, wet nuts and a cherry. Yum! How I miss those sundaes on the boards at the shore!

We finished our meal and Dad paid the check. Cash was the way, as credit card use wasn't wide spread back then. The only generally known plastic was a new and novel thing called Tupperware. Off we went, south on the boardwalk toward the amusements. We stopped in the drug stores and looked at the "T" shirts and sundries. Mom bought real suntan lotion for us kids. Dad waited outside watching the people go by. I looked at the risqué novelties in the window. We came to an arcade and wandered in to play skee-ball, pokeno, pinball and a few other arcade games. Each one was a nickel a play. Each one paid winnings in paper tickets redeemable for prizes at the main counter. The prizes were dolls, small balsa wood airplanes that required minimal assembly and really flew, puzzles, books and the like. Gambling was forbidden in those days. Governments hadn't figured out how much money they could make yet!

Finally, we arrived at the amusement pier. A pier built out over the sandy beach and part of the water (from the boardwalk). Admission to the pier was free, but each ride was individually priced at so many tickets a ride. Dad purchased a packet of tickets for us and we proceeded to the rides. There was the Tilt-a-Whirl, Crazy Cups, Wild Mouse – a roller coaster ride, Merry-Go-Round and many more all crammed onto the pier. We went on the Merry-Go-Round first. It was an uneventful ride. I liked to get off while it was slowing down to show off my physical skills. Of course, no one cared.

Next I went on the Tilt-a-Whirl, a ride that had small turning gondolas that seated three on a side and turned by pulling on a stationary wheel attached to a steel post mounted in the center. The entire platform holding all the gondolas rotated, too. I got on with several older teenage boys. They started pulling on the center wheel and turning the gondola as fast as they could make it go even before the ride started. Then, the ride began. The gondolas turned. The platform spun and suddenly went up and down at a steep angle very quickly. I must have looked really ill to Dad, who made the operator stop the ride, and got me off. Mom said I was as white as a ghost and was I ever dizzy and nauseous! It took the rest of the evening for me to recover. No more rides for me that evening.

Ed and Janice had cotton candy, soft ice cream cones and other candy treats that little children love to eat. I wasn't up for any of it being ill from all of the whirling about. When we went past a store on the boardwalk that had a large display of candy corn in the window, I felt nauseous all over again. Not from the ride, but from a bad experience the Halloween before when I over did it eating candy corn. To this day, the smell of candy corn makes me ill. Sometimes, just the thought!

The lights of the boardwalk and stores made it look almost like daylight on the narrow strip full of people. The trams ran up and down on either side of center of the boardwalk. Rolling chairs pushed by young men, or in the case of the electric chairs, driven by young men, meandered up and down, as well. There was an unhurried feeling about all of the activity. The people were all on vacation and had come to relax and forget the hustle-bustle of everyday life.

The next day after breakfast, we went to the beach. I brought a kite and the sea breeze was just perfect for kite flying. I had 500 feet of kite string and was able to let it all out. It was neat to see the kite way up in the sky floating along in the wind. I drew quite a bit of attention from the other beachgoers for a short while. Not quite my fifteen minutes of fame, but it was a good feeling. Of course, reeling the kite in was another story. It took forever and was much more difficult than letting the wind and kite unreel the string.

I went up onto the boards after covering up. It was the law – you had to cover up your bathing suit and body. I was alone. Children were allowed to do things like that back then, as times were different. There were hundreds of people already walking up and down aimlessly enjoying the sea air and sunshine. A voice came over the public address system. "We have lost parents of a child." The voice went on to describe the child and explain where to go. The PA system was all up and down the beach and swimming area of the boardwalk. They never had a lost child, only lost parents. No one wanted to frighten the small child any more than they already were by being separated from their parents. Once, it was Janice who had lost her parents. A rather frightful experience!

The sun seemed unusually hot that afternoon. I was dressed rather sparsely, yet still overheated despite the cool breeze. The top of my head was quite hot. Suddenly, I was overcome with darkness, slowly lay down on the boardwalk and passed out. When I came to, people were just walking passed me and looking. No one seemed to care that I was unconscious lying there. I got up and walked over to the Kohr's soft ice cream stand where a young teenage girl was watching me. I asked her for a glass of water, which she promptly gave me. I drank it down, thanked her and went on my way. I was OK after the episode and continued to wander up and down the boardwalk – in and out of the arcades and shops. Later, I told my mother, who didn't think it was a big deal.

Not being a fan of the sun, beach or ocean, I didn't spend much time on the beach or in the water. Several years earlier I was sunburned over most my body while playing on the beach in the sand. I spent the first week after vacation recovering. I was bright red like a lobster and unable to do much. Showering was a nightmare and rather painful. So, I spent much of my time playing arcade games and watching old movies in the penny arcade on the hand cranked movie machines. I studied the operation of the machine as much as I watched the motion picture itself. The machines worked for a specific number of frames after inserting a one-cent coin, a penny, into a slot. They were from an era long gone – the early twentieth century.

I like to people watch. I found a bench in a pavilion along the boardwalk. I just sat and watched people as they went by. No two people looked or dressed the same. Some were eating soft ice cream or a soft pretzel. Some were smoking cigarettes, cigars or pipes. Some were just in a sort of daze escaping from the realities of every day life. People watching was fun and I learned a lot.

The week in Wildwood seemed to go by slowly, but, in the end, went all too quick. It was time to pack up, go home and get back into the scheme of things. Summer was ending and soon school would start. The thought of school was OK. The thought of homework was awful! The end of summer had arrived. Labor Day had come and summer was gone in the blink of an eye.

Mr. Gurley's Trains

Across from the back of our house and up a few houses, lived Mr. Gurley. Mr. Gurley was the manager of a nearby A&P supermarket. Once a week in the early summer evening he could be found in the back of his house washing his red and white Chevrolet coupe. He kept the car immaculate, washing and waxing it on a regular basis. Mr. Gurley was a quiet, friendly man, greyed and somewhat balding. Inside, in the unfinished basement of his house, was an extraordinary setup of scale model electric trains. There were O gauge and HO gauge scale trains along with a little trolley car arrangement. The tracks were on a platform built into the front of the basement in an upside down "U" shape. Connecting the top legs of the "U" was an operating drawbridge of open girder construction with a single track on it. Most of the layout being O gauge was set up as a freight yard and an outer circle that went over the drawbridge. The HO scale setup was a simple circle.

Of the many and varied locomotives, passenger and freight cars making up several trains, there was his pride and joy, an O gauge model of a Pennsylvania Railroad GG-1 electric engine complete with dual pantographs. It was an olive drab green color and run infrequently so as not to risk damage or wear. It was a very valuable and rare model engine. When telling other model railroad enthusiasts about the GG-1, they would drool with envy.

On one side of the basement was his workshop. There were old kitchen cabinets and drawers full of salvaged scale model train parts. His tools were carefully placed within arm's reach for convenience. There was a chair and a desk lamp for ease of work. The room itself was dimly lit, as it was the basement of the house used for storage, laundry, ironing and other utilitarian functions.

I would watch, for what seemed like hours, as Mr. Gurley worked on a passenger car or locomotive, carefully replacing parts, cleaning and adjusting the many intricate parts of the work piece. I learned a lot about the insides of model train cars and locomotives just watching with intrigue as he disassembled and reassembled them. It was a wonderful time well spent just being there.

Sometimes he would let me run the trains under his close supervision. It was a real treat. I was never allowed to turn the electric current up all the way. The transformer was turned on just enough to run the train at a speed comparable to the real thing. Making a train run off the track was not an acceptable mode of operation and could damage the train or layout. It was a large circle of track by my standards and allowed me to enjoy the trains even more.

On a few occasions I was asked to help in completing a repair to the train layout. I was allowed to climb up onto the platform, being careful not to step on the track, which had been cleared of rolling stock. I know Mr. Gurley really didn't need me to do the work, but it was quite nice of him to include me in the repair process. Of course, I used more of things than he would. His manually dexterity was far superior to mine.

When the light shone through the back door of his house when I went there, I was in a state of joy because Mr. Gurley was working on his trains and I could visit. I loved to watch as he performed his magic repairing model trains.

His one wish was to find a $ 100.00 bill rolled up in an old passenger car that a grandparent had placed there to surprise a child. There were many opportunities for this because he bought and sold used trains. But, it never happened. And, he surely would have attempted to return it, if it at all possible.

The Front of the House

Our house, being a typical Philadelphia row home in West Oak Lane, had a stone front with brick and a poured concrete foundation. The front had three sets of poured concrete steps going up to the front door. The first set of steps went up to a landing that connected the patios of the left and right house. We lived in a left house as you faced it from the street. The next few steps went up to a small patio and landing in between the fronts of the two houses and under the windows of the sun parlors and living rooms of each house. The third sets of steps were separate for each house and went up to their respective front entrances.

The sun parlor jutted out from the house and had no upstairs over it. Just a roof. In front of the sun parlor was a little patio between it and the rock garden facing the sidewalk and street. Mom made it into a rock garden with some greenery because it was shaded under the tree located at the curb and had no sunlight most of the year. So nothing else would grow there. Under the sun parlor and flush with its front windows were two windows to the basement. None of the sun parlor windows opened. The living room window was a double hung window. The basement windows swung up and opened to the inside.

Above the sun parlor and its roof were the set back bedroom windows in Mom and Dad's bedroom at the front of the house upstairs. They, too, were double hung windows like in the living room, dining room and kitchen.

An early picture of Janice, Irving (Dad), Sylvia (Mom), Edward (Ed) & Stephen (me) in the front a neighbor's house

When summer came, Mom would set up a small vinyl covered steel piped swimming pool on the patio and fill it with water from the hose. It barely fit with the chaise lounge and two chairs already there. We would don our bathing suits, wade in it and get cooled down. Mom soaked her feet on occasion. It was great! Of course, it was only about a foot and a half deep and about four feet square. But, we loved it.

In between our patio and the schoolteacher's house to our left, was a small patch of earth with some greenery. It was the location of a tiny little fence that kept getting moved to what my Mom or the schoolteacher thought was the property line. It was a classic property line dispute – screaming and all! I never understood what the big deal was. One inch one way or the other. It wasn't like fighting for water rights or a major parcel of land. But it went on for years.

There was a hedge across the front of the patio above the rock garden. It was constantly in need of trimming. It made a great place to hide behind when playing hide-n-seek. Or just a place to hide from the other kids and just watch what they were doing. Sitting on the patio allowed for conversations with friends and family walking passed. Mom often sat smoking a cigarette there. Frequently, friends, family and neighbors came to sit and exchange gossip. What great stories we children overheard without even having to eavesdrop. We learned the dirt about the folks who lived around us along with stories about our family members.

Grandma

When school resumed at the end of the summer, so did the monthly concerts at Pennypacker Elementary School. These performances were put on by an eclectic group of musicians who enjoyed playing for its own sake. It was not about the money. It was about having a good time and sharing the music that they loved. The conductor was our family physician.

My grandmother, my father's mother, met me in between her home and mine, usually near my elementary school at Haines and Ogontz Avenues. Like my mother, my grandmother never drove a car. We met around 7:30 on a Wednesday evening. The concerts began at 8:00. We walked and talked about many different things – family, school, Hebrew school, what we each did that day. Grandma kept tabs on every one of the members of her family and always talked about how wonderful this one or that one was. She never talked about you or your immediate family members. She talked about the other members. When she was with the other family members, she talked about you. This concept took many years for the family to recognize and understand. Many in our family didn't like or understand her ways for a long time. Once understood, things were viewed differently.

Arriving at the school, we found our way into the auditorium and sat down quietly. The soft chatter of the people, young and old, who had gathered created a low din. For me, there was excitement in the air. I didn't get to go to many concerts and hear live music - only with Grandma. Although I listened to Rock and Roll on radio station WIBG on my little transistor radio, a relatively new invention, live performances were a special treat.

The orchestra began tuning up. The strange sounds of the instruments always intrigued me. The uncoordinated notes played to get each instrument in tune seemed always the same. Not annoying, yet not quite right in my head - just an orchestra getting their instruments tuned. I would learn much later the whys and wherefores of the physics of sound and the instruments themselves. But, for now, this was the way things were. No one explained it. It just was!

The conductor came on stage to a hearty round of applause, bowing to the audience at center stage. He turned to face the orchestra, raised his baton, began conducting and the whole auditorium filled with the sounds of classical music. How wonderful it was to listen to Brahms, Beethoven, Bach and many more too numerous to recount. Then there were the pops, popular music performances interspersed with the classics. I got lost in the music. My mind would wander, but always listening to the music. Sometimes tapping my foot to the beat, sometimes just sitting quietly in enjoyment.

In between selections, the conductor spoke to the audience, explaining the next piece and some of its background. Often, he would discuss the composer's life at the time of the writing of the piece. Other times, just a brief note about an orchestra member's special performance in a just played piece. He made the music even more interesting.

All too soon it was over and the conductor passed a hat around to collect money. Just something to defray the costs of the orchestra. No set amount. Whatever you wanted to contribute. Grandma always put a dollar in the hat in appreciation of the concert and the work the men in the orchestra did. The collection wasn't much, but it wasn't about the money. Others put money in the hat as it moved from hand to hand. Those who could not afford a donation just moved it along. No one thought any more of it.

Grandma and I found our way out of the auditorium and the school. It was night and the sky was dark. The streetlights of the city were lit all over. We walked back, retracing our steps to our original meeting place. We kissed and hugged goodbye and went our separate ways home.

Visiting 6th & Reed

My mother loved to visit with her Uncle Nat and Aunt Lee. They were my Great Aunt and Uncle. They had a home in the back of the beauty parlor my uncle owned and operated at 6th & Reed Streets in South Philadelphia. It was a three-story walk up plus a basement. It was a typical corner property in that part of the city that had a storefront.

In the back of the store was a room made up as a bedroom. Aunt Lee was very ill and bedridden. Whenever we came to visit, she was always in the bed but greeted us excitedly just the same. She loved to see everyone who came to visit.

My Cousin George lived there, too. He was seldom home because he worked for the State (the Commonwealth of Pennsylvania), spending a lot of time in Harrisburg. He traveled to and from work in a really cool sports car – a roadster with a real leather cover to protect it when it was parked.

The beauty parlor had chairs like in a barbershop to move the people up and down as they sat getting their hair worked on. It helped the operator by adjusting the height of their work – the head and hair of the customer. I always wondered how the chairs worked. I thought the post part of the pedestal was very long. I would go down in the basement to see where it went. There was nothing. I had seen a cartoon in the movie theater depicting a barber's chair being jacked up several feet and assumed that the post went somewhere. Of course, being young and naive, I found out later that it was all self contained and that the cartoon depiction was an exaggeration.

I would play with things in the house and basement. Up on the third floor was a record-making machine. It actually recorded sound and made phonograph records. It had two tone arms – one to play a record like most record players and one very heavy one to cut the groove in a blank platter and make a recording. It was really terrific. The cuttings were pushed to the center of the turntable to keep the long thin stream of material from jamming the cutting needle or tangling in the other parts of the machine. It was another new and novel device to learn about. I wanted to take it apart to see how it worked, but it wasn't mine, so I didn't.

It was a great place to play. All of the rooms on the third floor were for play. No one seemed to mind all the running around the children did up there. It was a fun place to be!

Trains

Many a Saturday afternoon I found myself hanging around the not so nearby Reading Line train platform watching the trains go to and from center city Philly. Sometimes a friend would come, but most of the time I went alone. The station was in Oak Lane as opposed to where I lived in West Oak Lane. It was up 66th Avenue, across Broad Street (the longest straight street in the world at that time), past the Harold B. Robinson car dealership and showroom where there was a recording studio in the basement, a bit down Old York Road, which crossed Broad Street diagonally at that point, and all the way down Oak Lane, a narrow street. It was past the Oak Lane Branch of the Free Library of Philadelphia and down a stairway and footpath. Just getting to the station was an adventure!

It was a lot of fun listening to the trains roaring towards me and then hearing the change in pitch as the passed by and moved away. I later learned about the Doppler effect that explained this phenomenon. But, at the time, it was just fun to learn about it by just listening. Sometimes we placed coins on the rail so that when a train wheel went over, the weight of the locomotive or lead car flattened it out into an oval pancake shaped piece of metal. You could still see the structure of the head and tail of the coin. But, was it ever flat! In those days, there were no railings between the inbound and outbound tracks at the station. Nothing stopped you from crossing the tracks. Oh, sure, there were signs everywhere saying, "Do Not Cross Tracks" in black letters on a white background. But no one paid heed. People were always crossing over from one platform to another. This wasn't a raised platform station. It was ground level and you had to use the steps on the train cars to climb aboard the train.

When we didn't have coins to play with, we put small stones on the rail and watched them shatter and fly all over. Not big stones. We didn't want a train wreck. We just wanted to have some fun without any mischief. The stones were pulverized!

Sometimes a freight train went through the station. Freight trains didn't stop or slow down. Staying behind a bench on the platform kept us from getting sucked under the wheels, as we were led to believe. If you stood too close to the fast moving train, you would be sucked under the wheels and die. No one was interested in finding out about the afterlife or if the myth was true.

Being the weekend, there were few passengers getting on and off the train, but there was a schedule to keep. The trains were infrequent, but always came and went on schedule. The conductor of each train came down to the platform and helped many passengers on or off the train. Constantly looking at their watch and keeping vigil over the schedule, they kept the trains on time. If they were ahead of schedule, they would make the engineer wait a bit. If they were behind, then they hurried to get going again.

Only the freight trains had actual locomotives. The passenger cars were self-propelled by electric motors in the wheels called traction motors, which are still in use today. When a freight train came through, the locomotive was always a diesel electric. It had traction motors too, but they were much more powerful. Steam had long gone from the major metropolitan regions by then.

Sometimes I went to 30th Street Station in Philly. It was and still is huge. You could go down onto any platform then. There were no restrictions like today. Once an engineer asked me if I wanted to take a ride in the locomotive with him all the way to New York City. I got really excited. Imagine, a ride in a real diesel electric locomotive all the way to New York. He said he could promise me a ride all the way there, but I was on my own to get back. All I could think of was calling home collect and telling my mother that I was stranded in New York. I don't think I would ever hear the end of that. Much to my disappointment, I declined the ride. How I would have loved to do it! Oh, well. It was another 45 years before I rode in a diesel engine and I had to pay extra for the ride on the West Chester Line, which is a tourist ride running only once a month.

Can you imagine what would happen today to an engineer doing that? He would probably lose his job and end up in jail. Times were different then. No one knew or cared about those things. It was a fun time to grow up.

Halloween

Fall arrived and the trees were changing colors. The reds, yellows and oranges painted the leaves as the weather progressively became colder and windy. One by one the leaves fell from the branches of the trees and landed everywhere. They covered the streets, the sidewalks, the cars – everything. Walking through them to and from school was fun. As they dried out, they crunched under foot with a distinct sound. Swooshing as you walked through them when you dragged your feet just above the ground. The wind whirled them around like miniature tornadoes. It picked them up, spun them around and put them down ever so gently.

Some people collected the leaves in piles and burned them. This was long before ecology was a household word. The smell of the burning leaves was just grand. It had a unique odor that was not overwhelming or unwanted. Most people today have never experienced the smell of burning leaves. As I mentioned earlier, others just created the piles and wet them down with a hose to keep them from blowing until the city came to collect them.

Halloween was coming and it was time to think about costumes, tricks and treats. This year I wanted to do something different. It was a time of ghosts and goblins, scaring and

being scared. Most of the things people did for
Halloween were pretty much the same from year to year. I
wanted to do something no one else had done. And, I finally
figured out what to do. The fallen leaves inspired me to create
a ghost that would even scare the adults, as well as the
children!

I got an old sheet, some rags and a long piece of clothesline
from Mom's things in the basement. I stuffed the center of the
sheet with the rags and tied one end of the clothesline around it
to form a head. The body of the sheet flowed and in the dusk
and dark resembled a ghost. I threw the clothesline over the
lowest limb of the maple tree in front of our house. It had to be
around ten or twelve feet high. I buried the ghost in the dried
leaves on the front lawn and threaded the clothesline over the
top of the railing on the patio directly in front of our house. I
put it through the window and into the basement. Then I went
into the house and down to the basement where I could work
the clothesline and watch what happened.

The first victim came along in their costume carrying a bag of
treats collected along the way. As they approached the place in
the front lawn where the ghost was hidden, I pulled hard on the
clothesline yanking the ghost out from the leaves with a
rustling sound and up into the air over the lawn into the tree. It
flew up at an angle – whoosh! The child screamed and ran
away. It worked! Wow!

I went up and reset everything taking care to hide the ghost
well in the dried leaves. Even adding some to make the pile
higher. This time I went onto the patio. I waited for a few
minutes.

A dog was chasing our neighbor down the street - a teenage
tough kid from a few doors down - he was running at top speed
too! - and then I pulled on the line. Whoosh! Up went the
ghost. The dog yelped loudly and took off as fast as its legs

could carry it - forgetting the bad boy! Wow! It even scared the dog.

I did this several more times to other children and a few adults who were escorting the smaller kids. They thought it was just great and laughed a lot after they regained their composure. I had succeeded in doing something different for Halloween and had a lot of fun.

Later, I got ready to go out trick or treating. I got made up with an old shower curtain and some stuff for my face. I made a scepter out of aluminum foil. I was a king!   Mom made her annual speech about watching out for kids with a potato stuffed stocking used to hit you over the head. I hooked up with some friends and we begged our way around the neighborhood until around 9:30 p.m. or so. We would go back to the houses giving out money two and three times. Getting a dime for trick or treat was a really big deal.

I came home with ten or so grocery bags of candy. Because there were up to 30 houses on each side of a street and there was a street about every 150 feet going east to west and every tenth of a mile going north to south, there were a lot of houses to go to.

When we returned with our goodies, each time Mom would go through every item and throw out the things that were not machine wrapped. She didn't trust anyone who put in things homemade. There were always those nasty rumors of razor blades in food going around. Mom wasn't taking any chances. Mom allowed us to eat a tiny bit of the candy. She wasn't letting anyone get sick and have to take care of them.

The Upstairs

The second floor of our house was typical of a 3-bedroom row home. There was the front bedroom, which was the width of the house, considered the master although there was no private bath attached; the bathroom for all to use; the middle bedroom, once considered as the maid's room, but I never knew anyone having a live-in maid; and the back bedroom.

Mom and Dad had the front bedroom as was befitting our parents, the king and queen of the castle. Two windows overlooked the roof of the sun parlor out onto the street in front of the house. Under the windows was a radiator that had been boxed in with a cover. Mounted in one window was a room air conditioner, an expensive and relatively new way to cool down. Several years earlier Mom had a closet built in to one side of the room with sliding doors creating an alcove for her vanity. It was an expansion, of sorts, of the original small closet they shared. I have to admit, in retrospect, that it was rather cramped.

There was a four-poster bed, bureau, chest of drawers, vanity and two night tables arranged in a logical, functional manner. Mom had refinished the bedroom set with an eggshell white finish textured with cheesecloth. It was originally finished with a dark stain that made the room somewhat gloomy. Mom hated the dark color of the wood and wanted something lighter and cheerful. She worked for many weeks preparing the wood, painting and texturing it. She was quite pleased with her work when it was completed and loved the look.

On the vanity in the alcove were two dresser lamps that were seldom turned on. When I was younger, I had taken them completely apart, but was unable to reassemble them. Mom was, to one's disbelief, so proud of the work I had done in accomplishing their disassembly. To this day I do not know how they ever got reassembled. I do remember playing with them at one time while they were plugged in. I got one terrible electric shock while my thumb was inside the lamp socket checking out the tab at the bottom for the connection to the bulb. I didn't understand about the socket shell being the other conductor. Ouch!

There was a light in the center of the ceiling with the requisite light switch on the wall next to the door of the room for easy access. This was the light of choice when the room was dark.

Leading away from the master bedroom was a short hallway with a railing along the stairway that led down to the living room. Like the rest of the downstairs, it was carpeted wall to wall. It had a joggle caused by Janice's closet jutting into it. It was lit at night with a 15-watt bare bulb. The upper part of the hall was half the width of the house and ran alongside the bathroom and the middle bedroom that belonged to Janice. At the other end was the third bedroom that my brother Ed and I shared.

The bathroom, being next after the front bedroom, was tiled with small white hexagonal floor tiles and white square wall tiles. It had the usual bathtub with a showerhead and curtain, a sink, toilet and linen closet. Nothing remarkable or special. Just a bathroom.

The middle room was relatively square, with a window overlooking the space between the houses in the back. Under the window, encased with a radiator cover, was the radiator. It had a closet, bed, nightstand and a treadle operated Singer sewing machine. Mom used it regularly to mend our clothes. We routinely climbed onto it and jumped onto Janice's bed, bouncing up and down. We spent many an hour playing in her room that way. It was no wonder her bed was destroyed and, somehow, no one knew why!

The third or back bedroom was at the back of the house. It had three windows – two overlooking the side of the space between the houses in the back and one bay window overlooking the driveway in the back of the house. The bay window was situated between two closets, one for Ed and one for me. There was an uncovered radiator under the two windows. There were two doors to our room. One to the hallway and one to the middle room. In between the doorway to the middle room and the two windows was a student desk with a lamp and chair. I used to roll up paper money and hide it in the brace of the desk chair. I had my intercom speaker set on the desk with a single wire to the basement using the radiator pipe as the other conductor. It worked quite well.

There were two twin beds with a nightstand in between. On the nightstand was a model ship with sails. The kind you see in the swashbuckler movies of old. It has a Christmas tree-like bulb mounted inside the center down in the hull with a switch on the wire. It provided some light at night, but was hardly ever used.

I had a bureau and Ed a chest of drawers in our respective places in the room. We each had various special items on top of our furniture for display and functionality. Considering our age and size, the room was quite spacious.

Each of the bedrooms was carpeted with a non-descript rug of some kind. Floors never excited me.

Ghosts & Apparitions

Winter had come to stay for a while. The cold short days were a stark reminder that summer and fall were gone. School had been in session for some time now. Afternoons were still for play, but evenings were for doing homework. School was good for me. I enjoyed learning new things and liked science and mathematics related teachings in particular. I did my homework either at the dining room table or at Dad's desk in the basement. Hand written work was the order of the day. There were no computers as I was born 1945 BCE – before computer electronics. We had an old Underwood typewriter that was used by Dad to prepare invoices, but I wouldn't use this for another few years for doing my homework. Essays and reports didn't come until much later.

After homework, we watched TV. There were several programs on after dinner in the early evening for children. Westerns, Disney, Milton Berle (Uncle Milty to us) and a few more. Bishop Fulton Sheen was on opposite Uncle Milty and once in a while I would watch him instead. He was interesting and had great lessons to learn even though it was a Catholic program and we were Jewish.

We would sit in front of the TV on the living room floor. We sat there so much watching TV that we eventually wore out the carpet! Consider that we basically wore the carpet down to the backing and it was wall to wall throughout the house. It meant replacing all the carpet in the house! But... Mom didn't care. She and Dad had purchased carpeting made of a new kind of material called Nylon, which was invented by the Du Pont Company. It came with an unconditional 3-year warranty. It was supposed to last a lifetime. I guess a lifetime was just short of 2 years and 6 months. Mom called the company where they purchased the carpet. Lo, and behold, they re-carpeted the entire house for free!

Bedtime came all too soon. One by one we went upstairs and got ready for bed. We would run around in each other's room for a while before settling down. Sometimes we hid in a closet in my bedroom. No one ever hid in Janice's closet. It was considered inhabited by something we didn't quite understand. Someone or some thing lived in there. We couldn't see it or hear it. But we always had a strange sensation come over us when we went into her closet. We avoided it like the plague. Janice only went in it when she had to.

Once our bathroom time was completed and horsing around subsided, we got into our beds and started to go to sleep. Ed and Jan usually fell asleep in a reasonable amount of time. My bed was next to the door in the bedroom I shared with my brother. Ed was afraid of the dark and had to have a light on all night. The hall light, that 15-watt light bulb, burned all night. I wasn't even allowed to close the door to our room a little bit. So it shined in my face all night. In addition, being next to the door, all of the sounds from downstairs kept me awake, as well.

The night droned on. Mom and Dad came upstairs and went to bed. I lay in my bed wide-awake. The hours slowly went by. I never knew the time, as the only clock upstairs was the wind up alarm clock Dad used for his morning wake up. Finally, I fell asleep. I must have been sleeping for a while and then suddenly I was wide-awake again. I turned to look down the hall toward my parent's room. The stairs were on the left surrounded by a railing with the walkway on the right from my bedroom door, past Janice's and the bathroom to our parent's bedroom. The light was shining as bright as ever. To my absolute astonishment, there were two small boys making their way slowly towards my parent's room, straining to peek in without being seen.

I screamed as loud as I could. The two boys turned and raced down the hall holding the railing. They turned at the end and scurried down the steps into the darkness downstairs. It was one of the most frightening moments of my short life. I kept screaming.

Dad came running down the hall to see what was going on. My heart was racing. I told him what had happened. He raced downstairs and turned all the lights in the house on and began searching everywhere for the two boys. He looked in the closets. He looked under chairs and tables. He looked in the kitchen and shed. He went into the basement and looked everywhere. Nowhere were the two boys to be found. He checked to make sure all the doors were locked and, to his amazement, there was a fresh fallen snow all over the ground. No footprints. Not a one! Where had they gone? If the snow hadn't been there, Dad would have called the police. But because he couldn't find anyone and there were no footprints, he concluded that there was no one in the house that didn't belong.

Mom and Dad thought I was having a bad dream. I explained that it wasn't a dream; that I was wide-awake when I saw them. To this day, no one knows what actually happened. It and Janice's closet are just unexplained mysteries in life.

Chemistry & Glassware

In the area where there was a small bench with a chemistry set and glassware all set up, I made what were characterized by my brother Ed as stink bombs – actually a rudimentary form of black powder. It made a wonderful bang when struck with a hammer, but smelled terrible because of the disproportionate amount of sulphur in the mixture producing a smell similar to that of rotten eggs.

Of course, I performed chemistry experiments as shown in the booklet that came with my A.C. Gilbert chemistry set. Sometimes they worked. Sometimes they didn't. But, as my high school chemistry teacher later pointed out, experiments never fail. Experiments only ever yield results. It is how these results are interpreted that makes a difference.

At one point I was the recipient of glassware, apparatus and some odd chemicals from my cousin Lew who attended premed at Villanova University. Wow! Test tubes, flasks, ring stands, clamps, single and multi-holed corks and stoppers and a myriad of other paraphernalia to conduct experiments and have fun.

The booklet that came with my chemistry set had a section on glassblowing. I learned circular breathing and began to make various additional glass apparatus by means of glassblowing. I was not an artist. I was slowly becoming an engineer. I made pipettes, bent tubes and rods. All to be able to make wonderful fountains contained inside of the flasks and beakers my cousin had given me. I used glass and rubber tubing with pipettes to control the flow of water, none of which spilled anywhere. I had devised a means to keep it contained in the glassware and have it empty into a container on the floor. I had discovered the principal of siphoning and used it to make fountains inside of corked up inverted flasks clamped to ringstands, which supported the arrangement of glassware and tubing.

I needed fire to perform many of the experiments and glassblowing. One method of making it was by the use of chemicals. I had discovered from the TV show *Watch Mr. Wizard* and from my neighbor across the street which two chemicals to mix together that self-combusted and got hot enough to burst into flame.

Amongst the paraphernalia was a small train transformer used to make a copper wire glow white hot for starting fires. This served to light the alcohol lamp for the chemistry set and glassblowing by causing paper to catch fire first. There were no matches because I was too young to be allowed to have them. I used the train transformer mostly as it was less costly and only consumed electricity purchased by my parents. For me, it was free. So I had devised another way of being a pyrotechnic (or pyromaniac, depending on your view).

Fuller Brush Man

It was summertime once again and my older cousin Lew, who lived down the street and was the one who gave me all of the chemistry paraphernalia, asked if I was interested in helping him with his Fuller Brush sales work. He offered to pay me for my time and I graciously accepted. Spending money was always welcome and I had no problem with working to earn it.

I was put to the task of delivering Fuller Brush catalogs for my cousin in the Oxford Circle section of Philadelphia. It was about a half-hour ride from our location in West Oak Lane to get to our destination. I got up early in the morning and was at Lew's home down the street bright and early. We gathered up his things for the job and went on our way. I was dropped off at a specific location and given an area to deliver catalogs. I was to meet Lew at the Sunoco gas station on Oxford Circle around noon that he had showed me. Oxford Circle was just that - a traffic circle at the intersection of Roosevelt Boulevard and Castor Avenue. It was huge because Roosevelt Boulevard was a twelve-lane road divided into four sections of three lanes each plus a parking lane on each outer segment. Castor Avenue was a wide street, too.

I went about my job of putting the Fuller Brush catalogs in the doors and mailboxes of the assigned areas and kept a watchful eye on the time. Since we had arrived around 10:00 a.m., I had an allotted two hours before I was to meet Lew at the gas station. Time passed and I headed for the gas station.

I arrived about noon and waited for my ride. Time passed like I was in a cold winter storm. It just dragged on and seemed to last a long time. It was 12:15 p.m. Then 12:30 p.m. Then 12:45 p.m. What happened to my cousin? Did he have an accident? Did he get lost? Where was he? I had no idea where I was and began to get upset. I had no way to get home and no money for a phone call.

Finally, Lew arrived and I got into the car. Whew! Lew told me that I went to the wrong Sunoco station on Oxford Circle. There were two Sunoco stations and I was at the wrong one. I had no idea! I came to a Sunoco station and figured that I was on Oxford Circle and here was the Sunoco. I must be in the right place. But, I wasn't. Anyway, it was over and I would never make that mistake again. Off we went for lunch and continued the routine in the afternoon in another small area.

A week later Lew took me to the same area and we began the process of knocking on doors and talking with the women of the house. In those days, most women didn't work and were home all day. Some gave Lew an order. Others were not interested. When a woman indicated no interest, Lew asked to have the catalog back. He explained that he had to pay for each catalog and it represented a specific amount of money to him. Most returned the catalog. Some had already thrown it away.

It took a lot longer to go door to door and talk with the women than it took to deliver the catalogs. We only covered a small number of houses that day talking with the women, taking orders and collecting catalogs. It was all very interesting to me because I learned about being a Fuller Brush Man.

The following week I arrived at my cousin's home. After knocking on the door for some time, he let me in and asked me to wait in the living room while he got dressed. I sat down and quietly waited. Once more the time went by slowly. After about a half hour I called up to my cousin. No response. I called again. Again, no response. I went up to his room and found him sound asleep in bed. I called to him and woke him up. He jumped out of bed and began to dress. I went back

126

downstairs, sat down and waited some more. Finally, he came down all apologetic. We loaded the car and went on our way.

That day I delivered the orders and collected the money for them. I only could carry a few at a time, so I would meet my cousin at the end of each street and get more bags of orders to deliver. At one point my cousin told me that I was probably carrying more money that I had ever carried before. He was right, but I wouldn't admit it to him. I was a proud person and this seemed a bit demeaning to me. But, I got over it! I was working and making money. What did I care!

VTVM & Time Division Multiplexing

I was always interested in electricity and electronics. It was a great age to grow up in. Most of the impetus in the field of electronics was enhanced during the Second World War. It was now some time since the war had ended but the research and advances were growing by leaps and bounds. My enthusiasm continually increased even with my limited abilities to obtain things. I picked items like old telephones out of the trash, repaired them and put them into use in our home. Eventually we had a phone in almost every room. My mother was so proud of me.

When I was about ten years old, the brother of one of my friends entered the Army and signed up to learn electronics. He attended the U.S. Army Communications and Electronics Command School at Fort Monmouth, New Jersey. He gave me, through his younger brother, my friend, the booklets he obtained and used in his training. One of these was on a process known as Time Division Multiplexing or TDM. I read the training manual from cover to cover and digested everything there was to know about the subject from it. I furthered my education on the subject and on electricity and electronics in general by visiting the Main Branch of the Free

Library of Philadelphia and reading every book on the subject in the reference section. Because these were reference books, they were not allowed out of the library, so I read them on Wednesday afternoons during one summer after attending morning sessions across Logan Circle on the Benjamin Franklin Parkway at the Academy of Natural Sciences taking a series of summer classes. In the books that had exercises, I did every exercise problem and learned Ohm's Law and all of the basic mathematics required to work out various problems surrounding electrical properties.

It wouldn't be until 1974 - 1976 time period that I actually used the concept of TDM to design a method of communication as an alternate to Motorola's cellular telephone system and obtain a United States Patent. The patent has been a great credential, but was never fulfilled as I was an unknown quantity to investors and Motorola was a big company. Even though at that point in time the Motorola system didn't work, they had put $13 million and many years into the project. It eventually became the car phone and now the cell phone system worldwide that we know and love today. While the problems prevailed, my patent was discussed on the floor of Congress as an alternative method.

Using some of the money I earned working for my cousin Lew and my father, I purchased via mail order a vacuum tube voltmeter or VTVM from a Heathkit catalog. I couldn't wait until it arrived. Finally, it came and I became even more excited. I opened it up and read the entire instruction manual, as was suggested, before beginning the assembly of my new meter. The booklet of instructions had places to put checkmarks as each step was completed. I learned the fine art of soldering as shown in the instructions and was very careful using a soldering iron I had been given.

Soon the VTVM was assembled and the next step was to plug it into the 110-volt outlet in the wall, turn it on and calibrate it.

Everything went like clockwork and the meter worked perfectly! Boy, was I ever surprised. I expected it would all go up in smoke because I miswired something. But I did it all correct and it worked! It worked well and I had assembled it.

I used the meter for many years to come. Even for a long while during the years I spent fixing radios, televisions and other electronic and electrical equipment in my early and young adult years. It gave me great pleasure.

The Prince and the Pauper

When I was in the sixth grade, our teacher wanted to put on a class play. She was known for her class plays by all of the people in the school. They were always elaborate and wonderful. This year her class would put on the classic play of *The Prince and the Pauper*.

I worked with a classmate to learn the lead role. We were good friends and both wanted the lead role. So we worked together to learn all the lines and practice acting. We used his wire recorder to record our voices and practice our lines. Being of the ilk of finding things electromechanical interesting, I was amazed by this device. It preceded the reel-to-reel tape recorder that was quite common then. When the wire used for recording would break, he simply tied the broken ends together in a knot, trimmed the loose ends and set it back to work. I was amazed!

My classmate and I were the only ones to try out for the lead role. No one else wanted it. I got the lead role. My friend was eliminated because he didn't turn in several days' worth of homework and had fallen behind the class in his studies. He was seriously disappointed. I was quite happy.

I also did all the lighting at the same time as performing the lead role. Another classmate who had visited my home and played with my space ship lights in the basement along with my trains and other things, jumped out of his seat when the teacher asked for someone to handle the lighting. He shouted that everyone should see what I did in my basement and that I should be the one to do the lighting. I got the job!

The play went off without much difficulty when we put on the performance. We all worked very hard. The entire class participated in one way or another. The audience included the upper grades and many of our parents and their adult friends. My mother and my Aunt Pearl came to see the play. They were so proud of me - especially my mother.

Radio and TV Repair

Prior to obtaining an intercom from my father's boss, I was going around trying to get one. I even tried to build one based on the diagram on the bottom of our new phonograph. The entire schematic diagram of the electronics was there! I started out with a diode and an electrolytic capacitor and some resistors to assemble a power supply. I had much difficulty because I didn't understand what I was doing.

As a result of visiting a couple of places to obtain parts, I befriended Walt, the manager of the radio and TV repair shop across from my elementary school. He hired me to work on Saturdays removing and re-installing automobile radios. I was paid the great sum of lunch because he was not authorized to actually hire anyone. Nevertheless, I work diligently and in return for my efforts, Walt taught me electronics and how to repair car radios and appliances. It was a great time.

I worked one entire summer for lunches only in the back TV repair shop and learned television electronics and repair. As my skills increased, I was paid the sum of twenty-five cents an hour for my time. I had achieved recognition and the owner of the company agreed to this vast wage!

I worked there for a long time and learned quite a bit. I ended up working for the company off and on for many years to come – through junior high, high school and college.

I was allowed to fix televisions that were abandoned because the original owners considered them too expensive to repair. I acquired six TVs over a period of a few years and made them fully functional. I brought them home and, eventually, we had a TV in every room of our home. My mother was so proud. In an era when most people only had one TV, we had seven!

Things are Different Now

Oh, the fun we had in the dark in the back bedroom! We had a little thumb sized toy light bulb made with phosphorus, which, when held close to a real light bulb for a few moments, would then glow in the dark. We played all kinds of games in the dark with this simple and inexpensive little toy! Imagine that - no batteries!

Mom's vanity table had a really cool little stool. It was bright blue and had a sort of Formica surface on the part that you sat on. It was quite slippery and we used to sit on it and spin and spin. No, the seat didn't spin. Our little butts did all of the spinning. We had contests to see who could get the most revolutions. We would spin to see who could get the dizziest!

The 4-poster bed was also a swell toy. The posts at the bottom of the bed served for great amusement because we would hang on and spin around the posts pretending to be acrobats of sorts.

It is so interesting to reflect on what we did as children to amuse ourselves - household furnishings, outdoor nature and construction served to occupy all of our time. Chases around dining tables, spinning on 4-poster beds, building snow forts, playing in and with piles of leaves or even puddles, playing street games like hide 'n seek or red light green light and all without much supervision or store bought toys!

Not only is childhood different now, but life surely changed for the three siblings, who spent their childhood days and lazy summers growing up in West Oak Lane. It was so much fun in retrospect wandering the streets on roller skates, bikes, sleds or just on foot – there were always some kids out playing that you could join – or – argue with! Of course, we were easily entertained by just chasing each other around the dining room table, too! Afterwards, the family moved to what we thought of as suburbia (though still in the city) and things would never be same.

Memories of Mom

My relationship with my mother was very special, as are most mother child relationships. In my toddler years, she nurtured me. I would lie on the bed or sofa and she would pat my behind to calm me down and soothe me. As I got older, she would tell me stories of her childhood and youth in a reminiscent manner. She taught me many things and kept me protected from the world and myself.

Because the times were less fearful, she let me be on my own from a very early age. I was allowed to play outside and wander around within specified limits from the age of three. By kindergarten, I was allowed to go to and from school on my own. By the age of seven, I was traveling the Broad Street Subway by myself and babysitting for my younger brother and sister. They lock you up for allowing these things today.

Mom played dumb at times and asked me questions to test my knowledge. We talked at great length about mundane worldly things. Because my mother did not understand technical things, from my elementary school years on, when I did technical stuff, we never talked about it. When family and friends asked what I was going to do when I grew up, she would jump in and say, "Computers!" Computers were new and novel in the 1950s. A veritable marvel from any viewpoint.

Mom encouraged me to do things. I was a free spirit. Free to do just about anything I wanted. I was basically an unsupervised child who was trusted. What did she know about my escapades? I seemingly never got into trouble except for the occasional (snicker) spat with my brother Ed. We would fight tooth and nail. On occasion each of us got in trouble over it, but not too often. We didn't tell on one another unless it was really, really bad. My sister, Janice, and I never fought.

Mom was always proud of her children - not just me, all of her children. It didn't matter whether we were always good or not. No matter what we did, she took the time to pay attention and boast about it. She was always telling someone about what one of us did or accomplished. She was so proud of us!